create je

stones

create jewelry
stones

Marlene Blessing and Jamie Hogsett

INTERWEAVE
interweavebooks.com

For my dad, Ron Hogsett, who was the first
to teach me about stones. —*JH*
For Deborah, sister and muse. —*MB*

All designs and instructions, Jamie Hogsett
All narrative text, Marlene Blessing
Photography, Joe Coca
Illustrations, Bonnie Brooks
Cover and interior design, Paulette Livers
Photo art direction, Connie Poole

Interweave Press LLC
201 East Fourth Street
Loveland, CO 80537-5655 USA
interweavebooks.com

Printed in China by Asia Pacific Offset.

Library of Congress Cataloging-in-Publication Data
Blessing, Marlene, 1947-
  Create jewelry : stones : stunning designs to make and wear / Marlene
Blessing and Jamie Hogsett, authors.
    p. cm.
  Includes bibliographical references and index.
  ISBN 978-1-59668-068-5 (pbk. : alk. paper) 1. Jewelry making. 2. Precious
stones. I. Hogsett, Jamie, 1978- II. Title.
  TT212.B568 2008
  739.27--dc22
                        2008003844

10 9 8 7 6 5 4 3 2 1

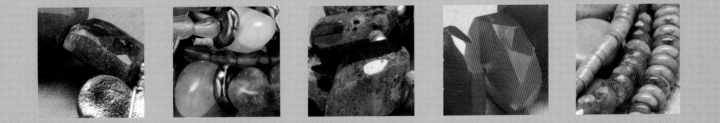

Stones: Earth's Timeless Treasures, 6

Stone Basics, 8

Techniques and Findings, 108

Project Resources, 116

Related Reading, 118

Index, 119

Stones

Earth's Timeless Treasures

Imagine an ancient caravan, journeying through the barren and mountainous terrain of western Asia to the Mediterranean. Traders and their pack animals carry raw materials—perhaps copper or gold, as well as turquoise and lapis lazuli—along with tools and finished beads. They are headed for Mesopotamia, known today as Iraq and northern Syria. Their transported treasures, particularly the uncut stones and finished beads, are amulets for those wealthy enough to buy them. They are also status symbols, reflecting the power of one who can possess such beautiful rarities.

The first humans who discovered colorful gemstones in the gravels of a riverbed or embedded in an otherwise ordinary stone must have been struck with awe and wonder. Such beauty, such extraordinary richness. It is not surprising that these stones were seen as magical protection, a source of various kinds of healing, an earthly treasure attributable to the gods, gems to covet or die for. The ability of stones to capture our imaginations and desires is testament to their staying power. By adding a few or many semiprecious stones to our own jewelry designs—be they turquoise, amethyst, jasper, or onyx, or any of the tens of stones commonly available today—we can either punctuate or entirely shape the look and feel of a piece.

Fast-forward to Audrey Hepburn playing the part of Holly Golightly in *Breakfast at Tiffany's*. Gazing into the legendary store's window in New York, this kooky party girl wants to be showered with gifts of the gem-encrusted jewelry she sees on display. *Breakfast at Tiffany's* describes an aspiration and a sense of wonder that has traveled through time from that ancient caravan and its cargo to the present. Lovely stones, whether they are precious diamonds or semiprecious garnets, still hold our fascination. We desire them. And, after millennia, we continue to romance the stones! For every occasion, whether you want to create a necklace with **Classic** appeal, a bracelet with **Special-Occasion** flair, or a **Fashion-Forward** pair of earrings that have head-turning edge, you will find jewelry designs, stunning photography, and clear instructions in the pages ahead that will help you make a signature statement with gorgeous, affordable gemstones.

Stone Basics

Wherever civilization has flourished, precious and semi-precious stones serve as a window into these cultures that have found, treasured, and made beautiful artifacts with them. Ancient Incan rulers, Babylonian priests, Egyptian pharaohs, the wives of Roman generals, Indian potentates, and Phoenician traders are just a few of the earliest lovers of stones.

For those who make jewelry, today's broad marketplace offers some exquisite stone beads and cabochons, many of them discovered in modern times, such as tanzanite. There are even non-precious varieties of diamond, ruby, emerald, and sapphire beads to be found. (Although, as you would expect, they are usually priced at a premium.) While it is true that the highest-quality gemstones are reserved for use in fine jewelry—think Tiffany & Co. on down the line to your local jewelry store—the semiprecious stones used for beads are still among the most special ingredients we can add to any jewelry design.

The information that follows is written more in the spirit of adding to your understanding and appreciation of stones than to giving you a gemologist's exhaustive knowledge of stones. That would require another book or two in itself! (See Related Reading list on page 118.) We also feel sure that, while it is interesting to know the facts and fables about stones, your passion for them will continue to be based primarily on the same thing that first drew prehistoric peoples to the bright, colorful stones that shone on the Earth's surface—their irresistible beauty.

What Is the Difference Between Precious and Semiprecious Stones?

Unsurpassed beauty, durability, and rarity are the qualities that distinguish precious stones (diamonds, rubies, emeralds, and sapphires) from their semiprecious relatives. These "Fab Four" of the gemstone world are all stones that are extremely hard and that, when cut, exhibit outstanding color and reflective brilliance. Certain semiprecious stones can be confused with them (such as blue spinel for blue sapphire), but when looked at under a jeweler's loupe, their crystalline structures give them away as something other than the real gem.

What Are the Basic Kinds of Semiprecious Stones?

Semiprecious stones fall into three categories: mineral, organic, and synthetic. A **mineral** is an inorganic (meaning nonliving) crystalline structure found in the Earth's crust. One of the most plentiful minerals worldwide is quartz, a relatively hard mineral that includes amethyst, citrine, aventurine, and more. **Organic** semiprecious stones are formed from living flora and fauna. Primary examples are pearls, amber, coral, and fossils. **Synthetic** stones are not natural minerals, although they are made with chemical compounds that grow real crystals. The best of these are virtually impossible to distinguish from the real thing—unless you're an expert.

Where Are Precious and Semiprecious Stones Found?

Stones of value are found throughout the world, with higher concentrations of certain gemstones occurring in very specific places. For example, the best rubies are found in Myanmar (Burma), Sri Lanka, and Thailand. Australia is the main producer of today's diamonds, with Africa still an important source. And so on. Gemstones form initially as mineral deposits in rocks. Each type of gemstone has a unique crystalline structure, which determines such things as the way and the degree to which the stone will reflect light (its brilliance), its hardness, and how it fractures when cut. The host rock is called the matrix. When the stones are mined, they are chiseled or blown from the initial rock formation or are found in the gravels of rivers and streams after having been released through erosion. When the latter is the case, the age-old practice of sifting for precious gravels with a sievelike device is still used.

How Are Stones Valued?

If you've ever shopped for a diamond engagement ring, you've probably heard the "Four Cs" valuation mantra: color, cut, clarity, and carat. These days, a fifth C could be added to the mix: certificate. This new C is especially relevant in terms of buying colored semiprecious stones. Because many stones are heat-treated, irradiated, or otherwise altered to achieve more desirable color, it is important to get a certificate from your jeweler authenticating that a stone is natural and has not been subjected to any treatments.

Ways in which stones are "improved"

Depending on a particular stone's characteristics and most desirable qualities, whether color, luster, or texture, a variety of methods may be employed to upgrade the stone's value. These techniques may also be used to hide imperfections. Heat treating, irradiation, staining, dyeing, greasing/waxing, or sealing more fragile stones with epoxy resin are the primary techniques. While you won't likely purchase gem-quality stones for your jewelry projects, you will want to know if the stones you buy have been altered. For example, those stones that have been heat-treated to deepen or change their color may fade over time or be damaged inside and fracture easily. (Note: The law doesn't require that a stone merchant mention that this process has been applied. A good reason to buy from sources you trust.)

The Mohs Scale of Hardness

German mineralogist Friedrich Mohs (1773–1859) developed a scale to classify minerals by relative hardness, with diamonds at the top of the scale at 10—a scale still in use today. In his "scratchability" test, each mineral can scratch those below it, but can only be scratched itself by a mineral on the scale above it. Minerals in the chart that follows are ranked from softest (1) to hardest (10). The semiprecious stones used in this book's designs range from 5 to 9.

MOHS SCALE OF HARDNESS	
1. Talc	6. Orthoclase
2. Gypsum	7. Quartz
3. Calcite	8. Topaz
4. Fluorite	9. Corundum (ruby, sapphire)
5. Apatite	10. Diamond

guide
to Common Semiprecious Stones

What follows is not a catalog of all of the many semiprecious stones available to today's jewelry makers. Instead, we have limited these descriptions to the stones used in this book's designs—the majority of which are the most readily available and affordable varieties. No doubt you will discover (or already have) that certain stones speak to you and are your favorites, whether you are drawn to their colors, textures, patterns, sparkle, rich opaqueness, luminescence, or other enticing qualities. Make your own substitutions in the jewelry projects in this book to create distinctive pieces that bear your "stone signature."

AGATE

This common, semiprecious type of chalcedony is primarily found in "banded" varieties—which means that the stone, when split open, exhibits concentric color bands. Most sliced agate sold today is dyed or stained to achieve bright colors.

Colors: White, yellow, orange, gray, brown, blue, or red

Hardness: 7

Sources: Found throughout the world, with major deposits in Brazil, Uruguay, Australia, the Caucasus, China, India, Madagascar, Mexico, Mongolia, Namibia, Scotland, and the United States.

Interesting Facts: More rarely, moss agate, a stone that has mosslike inclusions, is found. When cut, such stone does not have the typical banding patterns, but instead displays marbled or treelike patterning. In petrified wood, the fossil's organic matter is replaced by agate.

AMAZONITE

Named after the Amazon River, this stone's appealing color is due to its lead content. It is in the feldspar family, which includes moonstone, labradorite, and aventurine.

Colors: Blue-green

Hardness: 6

Sources: India is the major source of this stone. Also found in the United States, Canada, the former USSR, and Africa (primarily Namibia, Madagascar, and Tanzania).

Interesting Facts: When more greenish in color, amazonite can be mistaken for jade; when more bluish in color, it can resemble turquoise.

AMETHYST

This purple favorite is a member of one of the largest families of stones—quartz—and is found throughout the world. It is dichroic in nature, reflecting bluish- or reddish-purple highlights when viewed at an angle.

Colors: Deep purple, lavender, pale mauve

Hardness: 7

Sources: Brazil, the Urals, Canada, Sri Lanka, India, the United States, Uruguay, Germany, Australia, Madagascar, Namibia, and Zambia.

Interesting Facts: Ancients believed that amethyst guarded against drunkenness. Amethyst that is heat-treated becomes the golden yellow stone, citrine.

APATITE

One of the softer gemstones, apatite is often cut and polished into cabochons rather than being faceted.

Colors: Green, blue, violet-blue, purple, rose, yellow, and colorless. It can be transparent or opaque.

Hardness: 5

Sources: The largest deposits are found in Russia, the United States, Mexico, and Namibia.

Interesting Facts: The name "apatite" is derived from the Greek *apate,* which means "deceit." This refers to the way in which it can be mistaken for other stones such as peridot, aquamarine, or amethyst.

AQUAMARINE

This gemstone is in the beryl family—which includes the emerald as its most precious member.

Colors: Sea green, dark blue, sky blue

Hardness: 7.5

Sources: Brazil has the best gem-quality aquamarine. Other deposits are found in Afghanistan, Pakistan, India, the Urals, Nigeria, and Madagascar.

Interesting Facts: Most aquamarine on today's market has been heat-treated, turning green varieties to the more popular blue.

CARNELIAN

Iron oxide is the source of this translucent stone's rich coloration. It is in the chalcedony family.

Colors: Blood red to reddish-orange

Hardness: 7

Sources: India, Brazil, Scotland, and the United States.

Interesting Facts: Most carnelian on today's market is stained chalcedony from Uruguay or Brazil. Red agate is also sometimes sold as carnelian. To distinguish agate from carnelian, note that the former has stripes rather than clouds of color.

CHRYSOPRASE

Nickel gives this most valuable member of the chalcedony family its lovely green hue.

Color: Apple green

Hardness: 7

Sources: Poland, Czech Republic, Australia, Brazil, the Urals, Austria, and the United States.

Interesting Facts: Ancient Greeks and Romans incorporated chrysoprase in their fine objects. They also turned to the stone to improve eyesight and relieve internal pain.

CITRINE

Because naturally occurring citrine is rare, most stones in today's market are heat-treated amethyst. Like amethyst, citrine is a quartz.

Colors: Yellow to yellow-brown

Hardness: 7

Sources: Brazil, Spain, the Urals, India, France, and the United States.

Interesting Facts: Citrine was once called Brazilian topaz. While it is easy to mistake citrine for topaz (and some dealers sell it as topaz to increase its price), citrine ranks only a 7 on the Mohs Scale, as compared to 8 for topaz.

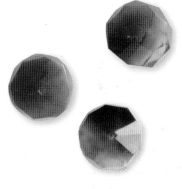

CORAL

A gemstone of organic origin, coral is formed from the skeletal matter of tiny marine mammals called coral polyps. Red is the most valuable variety.

Colors: Red, pink, white, blue, black, and gold

Hardness: 3.5

Sources: In the waters off Japan and Malaysia, off the coasts of Africa, the West Indies, Australia, the Pacific Islands, the Mediterranean, and the Red Sea.

Interesting Facts: One of the earliest stones used in jewelry, coral was often worn as an amulet. In Greek legend, coral originated from the drops of blood shed when Perseus beheaded Medusa.

GARNET

There are fifteen species of this plentiful stone. The most common garnet, a red variety called almandine, has been mined in Turkey since antiquity.

Colors: Deep red, pink, bright orange, orange-brown, yellow, green, colorless, black

Hardness: 7 to 7.5

Sources: Worldwide, with major deposits in India, Brazil, Tanzania, Brazil, Uruguay, Australia, and the United States.

Interesting Facts: Hessonite garnets, which are reddish-brown in color, are popularly called "cinnamon stone." The most important source for this variety is Sri Lanka.

GASPEITE

This lovely stone sometimes contains brownish patches, much like the matrix often found in turquoise. It is extremely rare, found only in a few locations around the world.

Color: Green

Hardness: 4.5 to 5

Sources: Canada, Australia.

Interesting Facts: Gaspeite is named after the Gaspé Peninsula in Canada, the first place where the nickel carbonate mineral was described.

HESSONITE GARNET

Manganese and iron inclusions give the hessonite garnet its distinctive coloration. It is popularly referred to as "cinnamon stone."

Colors: Orange-brown

Hardness: 7.25

Sources: Sri Lanka, Madagascar, Brazil, Siberia, Canada, and the United States.

Interesting Facts: In addition to cabochons and faceted stones, the ancient Greeks and Romans made cameos and intaglios with the hessonite garnet.

JADE

There are two types of the stone we usually think of as an earthy, opaque green—jadeite and nephrite. The more common of the two jades is nephrite.

Colors: Emerald green, white, lilac, red, orange, pink, blue, black, and yellow (jadeite); dark green to cream-colored (nephrite)

Hardness: 7 (jadeite), 6.5 (nephrite)

Sources: Myanmar (Burma) is the most important source of the jadeite variety. It is also found in Guatemala, California, and Japan. Nephrite jade is found throughout the world, with some of the largest deposits in Central Asia, Siberia, Australia, North America, Mexico, Brazil, Italy, Switzerland, Germany, Poland, and Zimbabwe.

Interesting Facts: For centuries, jade has been carved into sacred and artistic objects. Nephrite jade in particular offers a toughness that rivals steel because of its interlocking molecular structure. Thus, it was not only used for ornamental purposes, but also to fashion weapons. On today's market, a stone called "new jade" is not jade at all, but rather serpentine.

JASPER

A member of the chalcedony family, jasper is an opaque stone with beautiful stripes, circles, or spots. In fact, the name "jasper" is Greek for "spotted stone."

Colors: Brown and red are the hues we most often associate with jasper, but the stone also comes in shades from white to gray, pink, yellow, green, as well as mixtures of these colors.

Hardness: 7

Sources: Worldwide, although primary sources are Australia, Brazil, Canada, Egypt, Madagascar, Russia, the United States, and Uruguay. Red jasper occurs particularly in India and Venezuela.

Interesting Facts: Used for jewelry since Paleolithic times, jasper was associated with childbirth in several ancient cultures—particularly by the Babylonians.

MUSCOVITE

The most ubiquitous member of the mica group, muscovite is a very common rock-forming mineral.

Colors: Silvery, colorless, light green, rose, brown

Hardness: 2.5

Sources: Worldwide.

Interesting Facts: Some early windowpanes or "isinglass" were made from thin, transparent sheets of this mica.

LAPIS LAZULI

The stone derives its intense blue color from the mineral lazurite. The best specimens of lapis have glimmering flecks of pyrite and calcite.

Colors: Pale to dark blue

Hardness: 5.5

Sources: Afghanistan, the former USSR, Argentina, Chile, Canada, and the United States.

Interesting Facts: Ancient Egyptians and Sumerians especially favored lapis lazuli in their ceremonial ornamentation. One of the more famous pieces is the burial mask of Tutankhamen, aka King Tut.

ONYX

A relative of chalcedony, onyx is the striped, semiprecious variety of agate.

Colors: White, brown, black

Hardness: 7

Sources: Zaire, Namibia, Zimbabwe, India, Chile, and the United States.

Interesting Facts: The most common onyx found on the market is black onyx, which is often substituted for its more expensive look-alike, jet. It is traditionally used to make cameos and intaglios because, when cut, the exposed layers show contrasting colors.

MOONSTONE

This opalescent member of the feldspar family is usually cut en cabochon (shaped into a domed, polished stone) to capitalize on its shimmering quality.

Colors: White to bluish-white

Hardness: 6

Sources: Myanmar (Burma), Sri Lanka, India, Madagascar, Brazil, the United States, Mexico, Tanzania, and the Alps.

Interesting Facts: Not surprisingly, moonstone has been a favorite element of jewelry for moon worshippers through the ages.

PERIDOT

The distinctive green stone is the gemstone variety of the mineral olivine. It was thought by ancients to be rare, but is, in fact, found throughout the world.

Colors: Yellow-green to olive green

Hardness: 6.5

Sources: Worldwide the stone is found in Egypt, China, Myanmar (Burma), Brazil, Norway, Australia, and South Africa. However, the largest single source of peridot today is in the United States (Arizona).

Interesting Facts: The returning crusaders of medieval Europe brought peridot, then a precious stone with religious importance, back to central Europe. It was later the baroque era's most popular stone.

QUARTZ

Among the most common minerals of the Earth's crust, the quartz family includes countless varieties of stone, which range from transparent to translucent and come in numerous colors. Amethyst and citrine are among them and are described individually in this guide. Champagne quartz and lemon quartz are used in this book's jewelry designs. The stone is ubiquitous and affordable, found in every bead store's inventory.

Colors: One can find almost every color of quartz. One of today's most popular varieties is rose quartz.

Hardness: 7

Sources: Worldwide.

Interesting Facts: The name "quartz" comes from the Slavic word for "hard." It has proven extremely useful in technology (radar, telescopes, binoculars, etc.), as a central ingredient in glass, and even in landscaping as a groundcover material.

SAPPHIRE

Sapphires are in the same mineral family, corundum, as rubies. In fact, rubies are red corundum, and all other colors of the stone are called sapphire. The best gemstone-quality sapphires are precious stones, while lesser-quality stones are semiprecious.

Colors: Deep blue to lighter blue are the most commonly found colors, but sapphires come in a rainbow of hues.

Hardness: 9 (only diamonds are harder at a scale of 10)

Sources: Gem-quality stones are primarily found in Sri Lanka, Myanmar (Burma), Thailand, and Nigeria. A distinctive metallic-blue variety of the sapphire is found in Montana. Other deposits are found in Australia, Brazil, Colombia, Kashmir, Cambodia, Kenya, and Malawi. Large deposits of non-gemstone sapphires occur in India, Russia, Zimbabwe, South Africa, and Nigeria.

Interesting Facts: In the late-nineteenth century, production of synthetic sapphires began. Today, the quality of these facsimiles is so high that only by viewing the crystalline structure of a sapphire with a jeweler's loupe can an expert tell whether a stone is synthetic or natural.

SERPENTINE

Serpentine comes from the Latin *serpentinus,* which means "resembling a snake," perhaps because of its occasional spotty appearance. The stone is sometimes misleadingly sold as jade.

Colors: Green, yellow, brown

Hardness: 3.5 to 5.5

Sources: Worldwide.

Interesting Facts: Serpentine has been carved into decorative and useful objects for thousands of years. Ancient Minoans on the island of Crete favored the stone for such items as bowls and vases, as well as for seals.

SPINEL

Red spinel, which is blood-red in its coloration, has been called "ruby spinel." Chromium and iron are responsible for its red hue, while iron and sometimes cobalt give blue spinel its color. Transparent varieties of the stone are usually faceted as gemstones.

Colors: Red, blue, green, brown, and black

Hardness: 8

Sources: Myanmar (Burma), Sri Lanka, Madagascar, Afghanistan, Pakistan, Brazil, Australia, Italy, Turkey, Sweden, Russia, and the United States.

Interesting Facts: Spinel is often found in the same gem gravels as corundums (sapphires and rubies). The name itself comes from the Latin word for "little thorn," *spinella,* which refers to the sharp points on its crystals.

SUNSTONE

Also called aventurine feldspar, sunstone glitters from the reflection of light from tiny platelets of hematite or goethite within the stone. It can be faceted, but is often cut en cabochon.

Colors: Orange, red-brown

Hardness: 6

Sources: India, Madagascar, Norway, Finland, Portugal, Russia, Canada, and the United States.

Interesting Facts: "Oregon sunstone" is one of the few varieties of this feldspar that is found in gem grade. The variety, mined only in Oregon's high-desert country, also holds the distinction of being the only gem-quality sunstone in the world found with copper in it, giving the stone a distinctive coloration, ranging from pink to green or yellow to orange and red-brown.

TOPAZ

The stone's hardness, brilliance when cut, and variety of colors make it a jewelry favorite.

Colors: Clear, yellow, orange, pink, brown, blue, green, purple

Hardness: 8

Sources: Most important deposits are found in Brazil. Also found in Afghanistan, Australia, China, Japan, Madagascar, Mexico, Myanmar (Burma), Namibia, Nigeria, Pakistan, Russia, Sri Lanka, Zimbabwe, and the United States.

Interesting Facts: Blue is one of the most available topaz colors on the market and is made by heating the clear variety.

TURQUOISE

The earthy blue stone is one of the earliest semiprecious stones to be mined and used in ornamentation. Beads dating to about 5000 B.C. have been found in Mesopotamia (present-day Iraq). Coloration depends on the levels of iron and copper in the stone.

Colors: Sky blue to green

Hardness: 6

Sources: Iran, Egypt, Israel, China, Afghanistan, Argentina, Brazil, Mexico, Tanzania, and the southwestern United States.

Interesting Facts: Unaltered, genuine turquoise is challenging to find today. The porous stones may be altered by infusing them with wax or resin to create more vibrant hues and a smoother surface. Also, because turquoise is a relatively brittle stone, it may be impregnated with colorless or colored plastic, making the stone stronger and easier to polish.

VESUVIANITE

Formerly called idocrase, this stone was first discovered on the Italian volcano Mount Vesuvius. It can resemble such other stones as smoky quartz, tourmaline, peridot, and zircon.

Colors: Green, yellow

Hardness: 6.5

Sources: Norway, Austria, Italy, Switzerland, Russia, Canada, and the United States.

Interesting Facts: Because it is both soft and brittle, vesuvianite is seldom used in jewelry. When it is, it is usually cut en cabochon.

Now that you have learned the basics about the gorgeous stones used in this book, explore the photography and projects that follow. Discover which stones speak to you, which ones tell you they want to be crafted into a unique piece of jewelry. Whatever draws you to a certain stone, go with your response and start creating. These wonderful semiprecious stones will have even more magic and value after you have combined them in a stylish piece of jewelry made just by you!

the
projects

classic

As you finish wrapping the vintage blue vase, you imagine how beautiful this will look filled with a fresh spray of flowers from your friends' new garden. For the past two years, they have searched for the perfect starter home. Today you will join others for a joyous housewarming party for the excited couple. Before you head out, you'll also grab the traditional loaf of bread and bag of salt—guaranteeing a future of good luck and happiness!

Whenever you share one of life's important events with friends or family, you let them know how much you care by your gifts, your presence, and by the way in which you adorn yourself. After all, wearing something beyond the everyday sends a loving message: You honor them. Even if the festivities are casual, why not add a multistrand, opulent necklace of turquoise and muscovite to your simple white shirt and slacks?

Many such **Classic** occasions are, however, not casual at all. And it's very likely that there will be lots of photos taken to commemorate a housewarming or similar gathering. If you are sporting lovely hammered-silver earring hoops that are dripping with tourmaline and garnet dangles, you'll shine. A romantic lariat of peach moonstone and jasper is also a choice that will wear well over time and for many future celebrations.

Temple in the Clouds

MATERIALS

50 peach moonstone 10mm
    faceted ovals
2 imperial jasper 18x25mm
    faceted "clouds"
2 imperial jasper 20x30mm
    faceted "clouds"
14 borosilicate (boro) glass
    10mm rondelles
69 natural brass 3mm melon beads
2 natural brass 5mm square filigree
    bead caps
2 natural brass 13mm filigree cones
2 natural brass 1" (3cm) eye pins
2 natural brass 2" (5cm) head pins
2 natural brass 2mm crimp tubes
46" (117cm) of butterscotch .019
    beading wire

TOOLS
Wire cutters
Crimping pliers
Flat-nose pliers
Round-nose pliers
Chain-nose pliers

FINISHED SIZE
41½" (105cm)

Beautiful imperial jasper cut into this unique cloud shape and warm peach moonstone ovals are suggestive of a gorgeous sunset, while doubled-up brass cones and bead caps lend an architectural element to this long lariat. Handmade borosilicate glass beads bring out the greens in the jasper and tie the entire piece together.

1 Use a crimp tube to attach the beading wire to 1 eye pin leaving a ⅓" (.8cm) long loop. String 1 rondelle, 1 melon bead, 1 oval, 1 melon bead, 1 oval, and 1 melon bead twice. String one 20x30mm cloud. String 1 melon bead, 1 oval, 1 melon bead, 1 oval, 1 melon bead, and 1 rondelle five times.

2 String 1 melon bead and 1 oval twenty-two times. String 1 melon bead. Repeat Step 1, reversing the stringing sequence and attaching the wire to the other eye pin.

3 Use 1 eye pin to string 1 cone, large end first, and 1 bead cap. (Note: You may need to adjust the bead cap by gently spreading the sides in order to fit it over the cone.) Form a wrapped loop.

4 Use 1 head pin to string 1 melon bead, one 18x25mm cloud, and 1 melon bead. Form a wrapped loop that attaches to the wrapped loop on the eye pin.

5 Repeat Steps 3 and 4 for the other end of the lariat.

Good Fortune

A strand of faceted aquamarine rondelles goes from average to spectacular with a few small additions—different shapes of imperial jasper bring out its many color variations; herringbone stitched rings add texture and playfulness; and a ceramic scarab pendant, as a symbol of rebirth, resurrection and renewal, make this necklace a true treasure.

MATERIALS

534 dark green opaque luster
    size 11° seed beads
54 aquamarine 6x10–12mm
    faceted rondelles
1 imperial jasper 20x30mm oval
2 imperial jasper 20x30mm faceted
    "clouds"
1 porcelain 15x20mm scarab charm
1 sterling silver 30mm toggle clasp
2 sterling silver 2mm crimp tubes
2 sterling silver 3mm crimp tubes
20" (51cm) of silver .019
    beading wire
6" (15cm) of sterling silver
    22-gauge wire
Crystal FireLine 6lb line

TOOLS

Scissors
Size 12 beading needle
Wire cutters
Crimping pliers
Flat-nose pliers
Chain-nose pliers
Round-nose pliers

FINISHED SIZE

17¼" (44cm)

1 Use 3" (1m) of FireLine to string 12 seed beads, leaving a 6" (15cm) tail. Pass through all of the beads again to form a loop, then use the working and tail threads to tie a surgeon's knot.

Figure 1

2 Pass through the next bead on the loop. String 2 seed beads and pass through the bead on the loop again and first bead just strung (Figure 1). String 2 seed beads. *Pass through the second bead strung in the previous row, the bead on the loop, the first bead strung in the previous row, and the first bead strung in this row (Figure 2). String 2 seed beads and repeat from *. Pass down through 3 rows to the loop.

Figure 2

3 Repeat Step 2 twelve times (all around the loop). Use the working and tail threads to tie a surgeon's knot. Weave through a few beads to secure, then cut all tails (Figure 3).

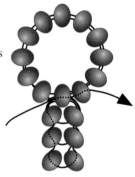

Figure 3

4 Repeat Steps 1 to 3 to make 6 ruffle spacers. Set aside.

5 Use the 22-gauge wire to form a wrapped loop that attaches to the scarab charm. String 1 seed bead, 1 faceted cloud, and 1 seed bead. Form a wrapped loop. Set aside.

6 Use the beading wire to string 1 crimp tube, 7 seed beads, the bar half of the clasp, and 6 seed beads. Pass back through the first seed bead strung and the tube and crimp. Cover the tube with a crimp cover.

7 String 1 seed bead and 3 rondelles five times. String 1 ruffle spacer, 3 rondelles, 1 seed bead, the oval, 1 seed bead, and 3 rondelles. String 1 ruffle spacer and 3 rondelles twice. String 1 seed bead.

8 String the wrapped loop formed in Step 6. Repeat Step 7, reversing the stringing sequence and using the remaining cloud in place of the oval.

9 String 1 crimp tube, 1 seed bead, and the ring half of the clasp. Pass back through the seed bead and crimp tube. Crimp and cover.

did you know . . .

Sealed with a Stone

For ancient Mesopotamians and Egyptians, stone seals were extremely important to establish identity. The seals, usually cylinders engraved with both a religious design and the name of the owner, were used to stamp transaction documents, from exchanges of land to letters. To do this, the cylinders were rolled over wet clay tablets on which a transaction was recorded. Signet rings were also used to impress the owner's signature. Seal-cutters were valued craftsmen, who kept registries of every signet ring they made. To lose one's signet ring was tantamount to losing one's identity! Stones that were commonly used to create the seals were jasper, peridot, amethyst, and serpentine.

TINY GEMS:

Ancients believed that aquamarine carved with the image of Poseidon would protect seafaring men. Another special property of aquamarine, subscribed to in the Middle Ages, was its ability to soothe the eyes. Thus, it was used in eyeglasses as well as in mirrors, the latter of which were said to offer glimpses of the future.

Modern Art

Organically shaped matte black onyx beads are fresh and fun in this no-clasp necklace. Their abstract cut is offset by the classic forms of the shiny onyx rounds and amazonite ovals. This is the perfect piece to wear as you cruise around on your Vespa!

MATERIALS

12 black onyx 4mm rounds

5 matte black onyx 30x35mm frames

13 amazonite 20x35mm ovals

2 sterling silver 2mm crimp tubes

2 sterling silver 3mm crimp covers

10 sterling silver 22-gauge head pins

30" (76cm) of sterling silver 22-gauge half-hard wire

18" (46cm) of black .019 beading wire

TOOLS

Wire cutters

Flat-nose pliers

Round-nose pliers

Chain-nose pliers

Crimping pliers

FINISHED SIZE

29" (74cm)

1 Use 1 head pin to string 1 hole of 1 frame and form a wrapped loop. Repeat with the other hole of the frame (Figure 1). Repeat entire step for a total of 5 wrapped frames.

2 Use 6" (15cm) of 22-gauge wire to form a wrapped loop. String 1 amazonite oval and form a wrapped loop. Repeat to make 2 amazonite links.

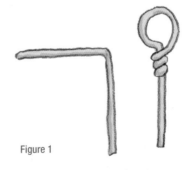

Figure 1

3 Use 3" (8cm) of 22-gauge wire to form a wrapped loop that attaches to 1 loop of 1 frame. String 1 black onyx round and form a wrapped loop that attaches to one side of 1 amazonite link. Use 3" (8cm) of 22-gauge wire to form a wrapped loop that attaches to the other side of the link. String 1 round and form a wrapped loop that attaches to 1 loop of a second frame. Use 3" (8cm) of 22-gauge wire to form a wrapped loop that attaches to the other loop of the second frame. String 1 round and form a wrapped loop that attaches to 1 loop of a third frame. Use 3" (8cm) of 22-gauge wire to form a wrapped loop that attaches to the other loop of the third frame. String 1 round and form a wrapped loop that attaches to 1 loop of a fourth frame. Use 3" (8cm) of 22-gauge wire to form a wrapped loop that attaches to the other loop of the fourth frame. String 1 round and form a wrapped loop that attaches to one side of the second amazonite link. Use 3" (8cm) of 22-gauge wire to form a wrapped loop that attaches to the other side of the link. String 1 round and form a wrapped loop that attaches to 1 loop of the fifth frame.

4 Attach the beading wire to the remaining loop of the first frame using a crimp tube. Cover the tube with a crimp cover. String 1 round, 1 oval, 1 round, 3 ovals, 1 round, 3 ovals, 1 round, 1 oval, 1 round, 3 ovals, 1 round, 1 crimp tube, and the remaining loop of the fifth frame. Pass back through the tube; crimp and cover.

did you know . . .

The Source of Serendipity

Arabs called the island of Sri Lanka, a major source of precious and semi-precious stones, "Serendib." This is the root of the word "serendipity," coined by English writer Horace Walpole in a letter to Horace Mann in 1754. His inspiration was a fairy tale about three princes who lived on an island where they frequently made fortunate discoveries by accident. Surely the beautiful rubies and sapphires that are still found in the gravels of the island's rivers can also be seen as "fortunate discoveries."

After hundreds of years, the riverbeds of Ratnapura in Sri Lanka still yield rubies, sapphires, and various semiprecious gems, which are sifted from gravels in simple woven baskets.
Courtesy of Rohith Jayawardene, Jayawardene Travel Photo Library

Tourmaline Sea

Top-drilled green tourmaline barrels and black silver leaves move like seaweed in this fluid necklace. With a slab of amazonite to anchor it all, the wearer will be transported to warm, flowing waters with this graceful piece around her neck.

MATERIALS

124 dark green luster size 15°
  seed beads
106 green tourmaline 2x6 to
  4x10mm graduated top-drilled
  barrels
1 black gold amazonite 20x35mm
  rough-cut slab
6 black sterling silver 8x25mm
  bamboo leaves
1 black sterling silver 10mm
  toggle clasp
2 black sterling silver 2mm
  crimp tubes
19" (48cm) of silver .014
  beading wire

TOOLS

Wire cutters
Crimping pliers

FINISHED SIZE

15" (38cm)

1 Use the beading wire to string 1 crimp tube, 4 seed beads, one half of the clasp, and 4 seed beads. String 1 seed bead and 1 barrel twenty-eight times.

2 String 1 seed bead, 1 bamboo leaf, and 2 seed beads. String 1 barrel and 1 seed bead eight times. Repeat entire step twice.

3 String the slab. Repeat Step 2, reversing the stringing sequence. Repeat Step 1, reversing the stringing sequence and attaching the wire to the other half of the clasp.

Opulent Cowgirl

Turquoise has the sort of élan that allows it to be elegant and rustic at the same time. Full strands of three different cuts of turquoise need only the small bit of sparkle from muscovite (also known as Russian sunstone) and smoky quartz to bring out their veining. This stunning necklace can be worn from working ranch to Rodeo Drive!

MATERIALS

271 smoky quartz 1–2x3mm faceted rondelles

157 muskovite 3–4x6mm faceted rondelles

16" (41cm) strand of turquoise 1x3–8mm graduated heishi

16" (41cm) strand of turquoise 2x3–10mm graduated rondelles

27 turquoise 8x10–20mm graduated nuggets

1 sterling silver 20x35mm 3-strand box clasp with turquoise inlay

10 sterling silver 2x3mm crimp tubes

8" (20cm) of silver .014 beading wire

TOOLS

Wire cutters

Crimping pliers

FINISHED SIZE

18" (46cm)

1   Attach 21" (53cm) of beading wire to first loop of one half of the clasp using a crimp tube. String all the turquoise graduated rondelles, 1 crimp tube, and the first loop of the other half of the clasp. Pass back through the tube and crimp.

2   Attach 21" (53cm) of beading wire to the first loop of one half of the clasp using a crimp tube. String all the smoky quartz rondelles, 1 crimp tube, and the first loop of the other half of the clasp. Pass back through the tube and crimp.

3   Attach 21" (53cm) of beading wire to the middle loop of one half of the clasp. String all of the turquoise graduated rondelles, 1 crimp tube, and the middle loop of the other half of the clasp. Pass back through the tube and crimp.

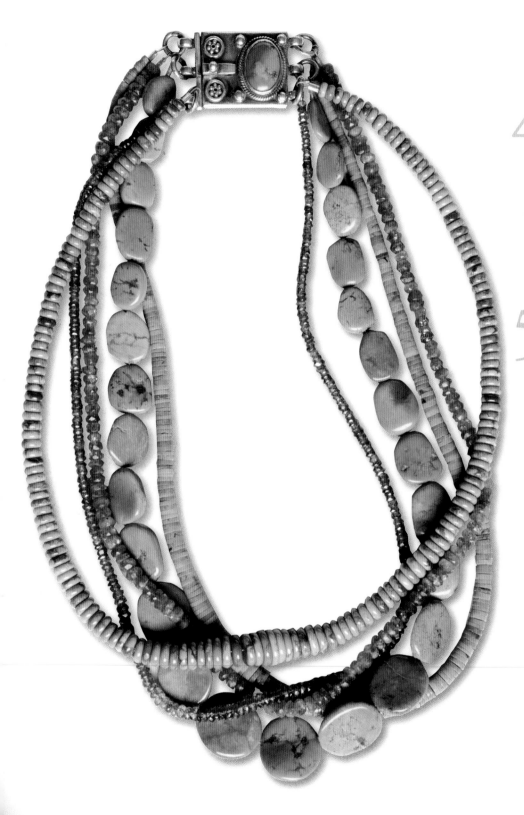

4 Attach 21" (53cm) of beading wire to the third loop of one half of the clasp. String all of the muskovite rondelles, 1 crimp tube, and the third loop of the other half of the clasp. Pass back through the tube and crimp.

5 Attach 21" (53cm) of beading wire to the third loop of one half of the clasp. String all of the turquoise graduated heishi, 1 crimp tube, and the third loop of the other half of the clasp. Pass back through the tube and crimp.

Developing the Lapidary Arts

Although stones were valued and shaped beginning in Neolithic times, the first lapidary work on gemstones dates to the seventh millennium B.C. in Mesopotamia (now Iraq). The earliest stonecutters had very basic tools, which they used to cut and polish stones into cabochons. The stones they worked with were the softer varieties that were easier to cut and carve, such as carnelian or turquoise. Faceting and polishing to highlight the sparkling light and colors of the harder gems did not develop into a refined art until the fifteenth century. In Renaissance Venice and Milan, the cities' lapidaries were renowned for their table-cutting technique, a popular style of the period in which the uppermost surface of the cut stone was flat (called a "table"). The closely held knowledge of these Italian craftsmen spread quickly to Paris, Bruges, and Antwerp, and later to Lisbon and London. Later styles of faceting evolved with ever more facets and shapes to capture the brilliance of stones. Patrons of the works of these fine craftsmen were primarily Europe's royalty, together with select powerful bishops and popes.

Lucky Strike

Chalcedony mosaics are reminiscent of old bowling balls, so they're perfectly paired with this bowling-scene toggle clasp. With the addition of red jade tubes and matte silver rounds, this is the perfect good luck charm. Its movement will ensure a perfect game!

MATERIALS

36 red jade 2–3mm tubes

18 chalcedony "mosaic" 15–20mm faceted irregularly shaped briolettes

16 sterling silver 3mm matte rounds

1 sterling silver 15x35mm toggle clasp with vintage inlay

2 sterling silver 2mm crimp tubes

2 sterling silver 2mm crimp covers

20" (51cm) of butterscotch .019 beading wire

TOOLS

Wire cutters

Crimping pliers

FINISHED SIZE

7" (18cm)

1 Attach 10" (25cm) of wire to one half of the clasp using a crimp tube. Cover the tube with a crimp cover.

2 String 1 tube, 1 briolette, 1 tube, and 1 round eight times, omitting the final round. String 1 crimp tube and the other half of the clasp. Pass back through the tube and crimp.

3 Repeat Steps 1 and 2 for the second strand.

Ring of Sapphires

Brilliant yellow sapphire briolettes of slightly different hues are stitched together to form tiny rings of sparkle. Strung with matte carnelian pebbles and finished with a charming box clasp, the sapphires gleam in this sweet bracelet.

MATERIALS

85 rose gold luster size 15°
    seed beads
104 yellow sapphire 3x4mm
    faceted briolettes
14 carnelian 6x8mm pebbles
1 sterling silver box clasp with
    mother-of-pearl inlay
2 sterling silver 2mm
    crimp tubes
2 sterling silver 3mm
    crimp covers
11" (28cm) of .014
    beading wire
13" (4m) of clear 6lb FireLine

TOOLS

Scissors
Size 13 beading needle
Wire cutters
Crimping pliers

FINISHED SIZE

7½" (19cm)

1 Use 12" (31cm) of FireLine to string 8 briolettes, leaving a 5" (13cm) tail. Pass through all of the beads again to form a ring. Use the tail and working threads to tie a square knot. Pass through all of the beads again. Use the tail and working threads to tie a surgeon's knot. Trim ends. Repeat entire step twelve times for a total of 13 rings.

2 Use the beading wire to string 1 crimp tube, 9 seed beads, and one half of the clasp. Pass back through the tube and crimp. Cover the tube with a crimp cover.

3 String 1 seed bead. String 1 pebble, 3 seed beads, 1 ring, and 2 seed beads thirteen times. String 1 pebble, 1 seed bead, 1 crimp tube, 9 seed beads, and the other half of the clasp. Pass back through the tube, crimp, and cover.

Sangria Dangles

Every woman needs a pair of hoops. This classic style is made special by wire-wrapped dangles of pink garnet and watermelon tourmaline. Like the fruity drink for which these earrings are named, they are quite tasty indeed!

MATERIALS

38 pink garnet 3mm faceted rounds

8 watermelon tourmaline 6x10mm irregularly shaped briolettes

2 sterling silver VEE-O Vogue 21mm rings

1 pair sterling silver ear wires with disc front

30 sterling silver 26-gauge head pins

16" (41cm) sterling silver 26-gauge wire

TOOLS

Wire cutters

Flat-nose pliers

Round-nose pliers

Chain-nose pliers

FINISHED SIZE

2" (5cm)

1 Use 2" (5cm) of wire and 1 briolette to form the first part of a wrapped loop bail (see page 115 and Figure 1). Use the straight-up wire to string 1 round and form a wrapped loop that attaches to 1 ring.

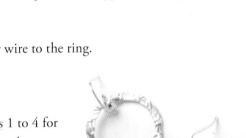

Figure 1

2 Use 1 head pin to string 1 round. Form a wrapped loop that attaches to the ring to the right of the previous loop. Repeat entire step five times for a total of 6 garnet dangles.

3 Repeat Steps 1 and 2 twice, placing all new wrapped loops to the right of the previous wrapped loop. Repeat Step 1.

4 Attach 1 ear wire to the ring.

5 Repeat Steps 1 to 4 for the second earring.

did you know . . .

Treasure Island

Sri Lanka, a small island off the tip of India, is known in both fable and fact as a place rich in gemstones. The adventurer and trader Marco Polo, together with his father and uncle, may well have been the first Europeans to visit the island in 1294 during their return from a China expedition. Previously, they had heard of the island only through stories. However, after encountering the true treasures of the mythic place, Polo wrote in his journal, "From its streams come rubies, sapphires, topazes, amethysts and garnets." (Some fascinating excerpts from Marco Polo's journal are included in the appendix of *Jewels: A Secret History* by Victoria Finlay.) In fact, Sri Lanka, once known as Ceylon, continues to be an important source of rubies and sapphires. Just as they have for thousands of years, locals continue to sift for the precious gems in the gravels of rivers with simple, open-weave baskets. The gems are carried downstream after they have been released from the eroded matrix in which they first formed.

TINY GEMS

The sapphire is the only precious stone ever to have been found in Britain.

Charlemagne's Legendary Talisman

In the ninth century, an Arab caliph presented Charlemagne, king of the Franks and Holy Roman Emperor, with a beautiful talisman whose central stone was a large sapphire cabochon. Believing it had miraculous powers, the emperor bore the treasured jewel to his grave in A.D. 814. Years later, when Otto III (A.D. 980–1002) had Charlemagne's tomb opened, the body was remarkably preserved, adding fuel to the belief in the stone's powers. In the nineteenth century, the talisman was presented by Napoleon to his consort, Josephine. Later, it passed to the wife of Napoleon II, Princess Eugenie. She gave it to the city of Rheims to help pay for the reconstruction of the city's cathedral, damaged greatly in World War I.

Royal jewelry often featured stunning sapphires, as in these pieces from Sotheby's Auction House.
Courtesy of Philippe Caron/ Corbis Sygma

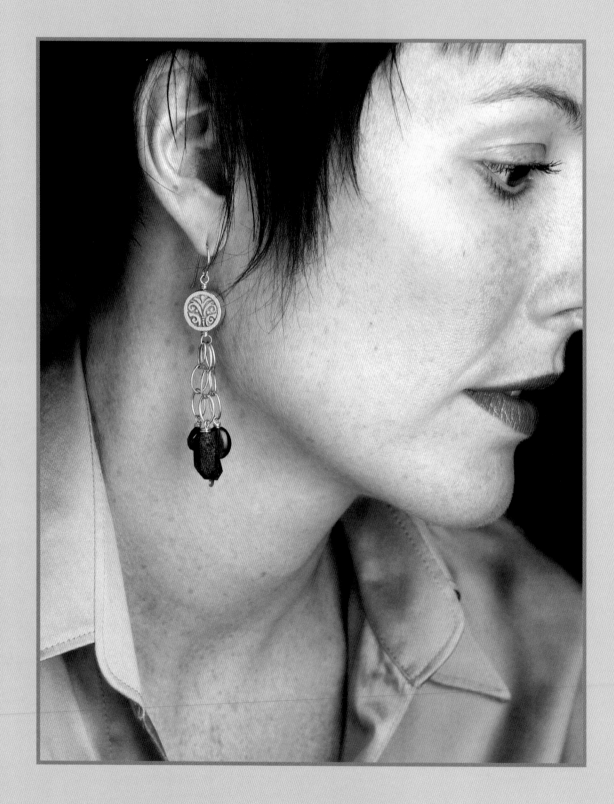

Swinging Mosaics

Decorated gold vermeil coins are the perfect anchor for three different dangling stones. The colors of garnet, amethyst, and thulite, in different shapes and sizes, blend together beautifully as short chains allow these earrings to move gracefully at the neck.

MATERIALS

2 garnet 5x6mm faceted teardrops

2 amethyst 6x8mm ovals

2 thulite 8x20mm nuggets

2 gold vermeil 12mm coins

6 gold vermeil 6x8mm oval three-link
   chains

1 pair gold vermeil ear wires

2 gold vermeil fancy head pins

4 gold-filled 22-gauge head pins

5" (13cm) of gold-filled 22-gauge wire

TOOLS

Wire cutters

Flat-nose pliers

Round-nose pliers

Chain-nose pliers

FINISHED SIZE

3" (8cm)

1 Use 2½" (6cm) of 22-gauge wire to form a wrapped loop that attaches to one end of 3 chains. String 1 coin and form a wrapped loop that attaches to 1 ear wire.

2 Use 1 fancy head pin to string 1 thulite nugget. Form a wrapped loop that attaches to the middle chain attached in Step 1.

3 Use 1 head pin to string 1 amethyst oval. Form a wrapped loop that attaches to one of the remaining chains from Step 1. Use 1 head pin to string 1 garnet teardrop. Form a wrapped loop that attaches to the remaining chain from Step 1.

4 Repeat Steps 1 to 3 for the other earring.

special-occasion

What could be better than a wine-tasting for a good cause? You bought tickets months ago for this gala at the new community arts center. The night will be festive, with glasses clinking, people murmuring about how dazzling the occasion is, how delicious the jewel-toned pinots, cabs, and syrahs are.

When you attend a special event, one where celebration is the underlying theme, you want to look special as well. Maybe that little black dress that always fits the occasion is just what you'll choose to wear. After all, the little black dress is always in fashion. But when you add jewelry with semiprecious stones to your outfit, you definitely spark things up a notch.

One great choice is a necklace that has dramatic patterned black circles as a focal element, mixed with the blue, green, and yellowish beauty of lemon quartz, agate, and chalcedony. Or if you want a touch of Asia instead, the soft pinkish tones of lotus jasper with lavender pearl accents could be the perfect necklace.

But maybe bracelets or earrings are more your style. Mix large, rough-faceted smoky citrine stones with blue-green apatite and vintage brass to give you a bracelet you'll love to display as you gesture animatedly. Another great choice would be some dramatic blue chrysoprase earrings, dangling from your lobes, making the statement: This is a Special Occasion!

Un, deux, trois!

Citrine, chalcedony, and agate string up into one necklace that can be worn three different ways! Use the S-clasp and wear the five agate coins in front. Use the round lobster clasp with agate dangle as a pendant and wear the agate coins at the nape of the neck. Or use the marquis lobster clasp with chain-dangled citrine and chalcedony as a front focal piece or a graceful dangle down the neck.

MATERIALS

37 lemon quartz 6x8mm faceted rectangles
44 chalcedony 6–6x8mm cubes
30 chalcedony 6x10–12mm faceted barrels
6 agate 30mm coins
2 matte silver 4mm rounds
1 sterling silver 12mm round lobster clasp
1 sterling silver 8x16mm marquis lobster clasp
1 sterling silver S-hook clasp
2 sterling silver figure eights
2 sterling silver 3mm crimp tubes
7 sterling silver 22-gauge head pins
3 sterling silver 24-gauge head pins
8" (20cm) of sterling silver 3 and 1 link chain
3" (8cm) of sterling silver 22-gauge wire
55" (2m) of .014 beading wire

TOOLS

Wire cutters
Mighty Crimper crimping pliers
Flat-nose pliers
Chain-nose pliers
Round-nose pliers
Bead stops

FINISHED SIZE

20" (51cm) with 2" (5cm) and 3¼" (8cm) interchangeable pendants

1 Cut the beading wire into three 22" (56cm) pieces. Use all three pieces to string 1 crimp tube and 1 figure eight. Pass the wire back through the tube and crimp using Mighty Crimper crimping pliers.

2 Use 1 strand of wire to string 17 rectangles. Place a bead stop on the wire.

3 Use a second strand of wire to string 21 cubes. Place a bead stop on the wire.

4 Use the third strand to string 13 barrels. Place a bead stop on the wire.

5 Remove bead stops. Use all 3 wires to string 5 agate coins.

6 Repeat Step 2.
Repeat Step 3, stringing 20 cubes.
Repeat Step 4.

7 Use all three wires to string 1 crimp tube and the second figure eight. Pass back through the tube and crimp.

8 To wear with the 5 agates in front of the neck, use the S-clasp to connect the figure eights.

9 To wear with the 5 agates in back of the neck, use one 22-gauge head pin to string 1 silver round, 1 agate coin, and 1 silver round. Form a wrapped loop that attaches to the round lobster clasp. Attach the agate pendant to the figure eights.

10 To wear with the 5 agates in the front *or* back of the neck, cut the chain into one 2" (5cm) piece, two 1½" (4cm) pieces, two 1" (3cm) pieces, and two ½" (1cm) pieces.

11 Use one 24-gauge head pin to string 1 rectangle; form a wrapped loop. Repeat.

12 Use one 22-gauge head pin to string 1 barrel. Form a wrapped loop that attaches to ½" (1cm) of chain. Repeat.

13 Use one 22-gauge head pin to string 1 cube. Form a wrapped loop that attaches to 1" (3cm) of chain. Repeat.

14 Use one 22-gauge head pin to string 1 barrel. Form a wrapped loop that attaches to 1½" (4cm) of chain. Repeat.

15 Use one 24-gauge head pin to string 1 rectangle. Form a wrapped loop that attaches to 2" (5cm) of chain.

16 Use the 22-gauge wire to form a large wrapped loop that attaches to one piece formed in Step 11, one piece formed in Step 12, one piece formed in Step 13, one piece formed in Step 14, one piece formed in Step 15, one piece formed in Step 15, one piece formed in Step 13, one piece formed in Step 12, and one piece formed in Step 11. Use the wire to string 1 cube. Form a wrapped loop that attaches to the marquis lobster clasp. Attach the marquis lobster clasp to the figure eights.

did you know . . .

Birthstones—Fixed?

Throughout the ages, particular gemstones have been associated with each of the zodiac signs. But it wasn't until a 1912 meeting of the American National Association of Jewelers that a formal list was drawn up, designating the stones we should each desire to commemorate our birth months. The designations weren't, however, mystical in origin. Like most trade association lists, this list was created to promote the sales of stones jewelers most wanted to sell. Interestingly, the list has held up to this day. In the future, the list may expand to include tanzanite, a popular gemstone that was only discovered in 1967. Below is the list as it still stands.

JANUARY • GARNET	FEBRUARY • AMETHYST	MARCH • AQUAMARINE
APRIL • DIAMOND	MAY • EMERALD	JUNE • MOONSTONE
JULY • RUBY	AUGUST • PERIDOT	SEPTEMBER • SAPPHIRE
OCTOBER • OPAL	NOVEMBER • TOPAZ	DECEMBER • TURQUOISE

Courtesy of American Gem Trade Association.

Heavenly Lotus

Large lotus jasper marquis feel light and airy when strung with green amethyst marquis and lavender pearls. The sections of green amethyst and pearls seem extra fresh because there are two strands of them between each lotus jasper. The back of the pewter pendant reads "enlightenment."

MATERIALS

108 matte purple size 11° seed beads

24 lavender 6mm freshwater pearls

24 green amethyst 6x10mm top-drilled marquis

6 lotus jasper 16x26mm marquis

1 pewter 18x25mm lotus pendant

1 sterling silver two-strand hook-and-eye clasp with pearl inlay

4 sterling silver 2mm crimp tubes

40" (102cm) of .014 beading wire

TOOLS

Wire cutters

Crimping pliers

Bead stops

FINISHED SIZE

17¼" (44cm)

1 Use 20" (51cm) of beading wire to string one hole of the pendant. Use each end of wire to string 4 seed beads. Center the beads and pendant on the wire. Use both wires to string 1 seed bead.

2 Use one wire to string 1 seed bead, 1 top-drilled marquis, 1 seed bead, 1 pearl, 1 seed bead, 1 top-drilled marquis, and 1 seed bead. Place a bead stop on the wire. Use the other wire to string 1 seed bead, 1 pearl, 1 seed bead, 1 top-drilled marquis, 1 seed bead, 1 pearl, and 1 seed bead. Use both wires to string 1 seed bead, 1 lotus jasper marquis, and 1 seed bead.

3 Repeat Step 2 twice, omitting the final seed bead, lotus jasper marquis, and seed bead. Use 1 wire to string 1 crimp tube, 4 seed beads, the inside loop of one half of the clasp, and 4 seed beads. Pass back through the tube and crimp. Use the other wire to string 1 crimp tube, 4 seed beads, the outside loop of the same half of the clasp, and 4 seed beads. Pass back through the tube and crimp.

4 Repeat Steps 1 to 3 using the other hole of the pendant and the other half of the clasp.

did you know . . .

Coeur de la Mer

On the right, the tanzanite heart necklace worn by Kate Winslet in *Titanic* hangs amid costume items and props from various films.
Photo by Annebicque
Bernard/Corbis Sygma

Vintage Vogue

Smooth blue apatite rondelles and spiral faceted smoky citrine give a modern edge to this antique-looking bracelet. Filigree bead caps and a leaf clasp in brass may appear old, though they are newly cast, and their patina brings out the color variation of the citrine as well as pairs exceptionally well with the opaque blue of the apatite.

MATERIALS

12 blue apatite 4x6mm rondelles

4 smoky citrine 10x20mm faceted ovals

7 natural brass 3mm melon beads

4 natural brass 12mm filigree bead caps

1 natural brass leaf toggle bar

1 natural brass leaf toggle ring

2 natural brass 2mm crimp beads

1 natural brass 1" (3cm) head pin

10" (25cm) of bronze .019 beading wire

TOOLS

Wire cutters

Crimping pliers

FINISHED SIZE:

8" (20cm)

1 Use the head pin to string the toggle bar. Form a wrapped loop.

2 Attach the wire to the wrapped loop using a crimp tube. String 3 melon beads, 3 apatite rondelles, 1 melon bead, 1 smoky citrine oval, 1 melon bead, 3 apatite rondelles, 1 bead cap, 1 smoky citrine oval, 1 bead cap, 3 apatite rondelles, 1 melon bead, 1 smoky citrine oval, 1 melon bead, 3 apatite rondelles, 1 bead cap, 1 smoky citrine oval, and 1 bead cap.

3 String 1 crimp tube and the toggle ring. Pass back through the tube and crimp.

Arachne's Treasure

According to mythology, the mortal Arachne turned into a spider after winning a competition with Athena, patron goddess of weaving. The competition was over who could produce the most beautiful tapestry, and the clasp of this alluring bracelet represents Arachne's tale. The bracelet's design is enhanced with three strands of blue apatite and hessonite garnet mixed with crystals.

1 Attach 10" (25cm) of wire to one half of the clasp using a crimp tube. String 1 light sapphire brandy bicone, 1 coin, 1 light sapphire brandy bicone, 1 rondelle, 1 crystal ice bicone, 1 nugget, 1 crystal ice bicone, and 1 rondelle three times, omitting the final rondelle. String 1 crimp tube and the other half of the clasp. Pass back through the tube and crimp.

MATERIALS

16 blue apatite 4x6mm rondelles

9 blue apatite 16mm coins

9 hessonite garnet 10x12–13x20mm nuggets

18 light sapphire brandy 4mm crystal bicones

19 crystal ice 4mm crystal bicones

1 sterling silver with vintage cabochon 20x25mm box clasp

6 sterling silver 2mm crimp tubes

30" (76cm) of silver .014 beading wire

TOOLS

Wire cutters

Magical Crimp Forming pliers or crimping pliers

FINISHED SIZE

8" (20cm)

2 Attach 10" (25cm) of wire to one half of the clasp using a crimp tube. String 1 crystal ice bicone, 1 nugget, 1 crystal ice bicone, 1 rondelle, 1 light sapphire brandy bicone, 1 coin, 1 light sapphire brandy bicone, and 1 rondelle three times, omitting the final rondelle. String 1 crimp tube and the other half of the clasp. Pass back through the tube and crimp.

3 Attach 10" (25cm) of wire to one half of the clasp using a crimp tube. String 1 crystal ice bicone and 1 rondelle. String 1 light sapphire brandy bicone, 1 coin, 1 light sapphire brandy bicone, 1 rondelle, 1 crystal ice bicone, 1 nugget, 1 crystal ice bicone, and 1 rondelle three times, omitting the final rondelle. String 1 crimp tube and the other half of the clasp. Pass back through the tube and crimp.

TINY GEMS

Because apatite embedded in marine deposits contains phosphorus, it is mined for use in matches.

did you know . . .

Why a Carat?

In modern times, this measure of a gemstone's weight represents .20 gram. However, like most measures, it was derived from a much less abstract concept. In the markets of the Middle East and Asia, ancient jewelers trading in expensive gems chose carob seeds to measure stone weights. They did this because the seeds were relatively uniform and could therefore be counted on for a high degree of accuracy when weighing precious stones on a scale. However, this measure was still approximate, and in the nineteenth century, European gem merchants began working to agree on a more standardized measure—one that would be the same no matter where in the world a gem was weighed. It wasn't until the early twentieth century that a final agreed-upon measure—.20 gram per carat—was accepted in both Europe and the United States.

Twilight Flight

Gold vermeil links resembling twigs and birds need only a small strand of lapis lazuli briolettes to become a showstopping necklace. The shiny gold findings bring out the brilliant blue of the lapis, a stone whose modern name originates from the Persian word *lazhuward,* meaning "blue," and the Arabic word *lazaward,* meaning "heaven" or "sky."

MATERIALS

61 lapis lazuli graduated 4x6–
    6x8mm briolettes
2 gold vermeil 8x20mm bird links
5 gold vermeil 4x40mm twig links
1 gold vermeil 10x15mm marquis
    toggle clasp
16 gold-filled 2mm crimp tubes
26" (66cm) of 24k gold .014
    beading wire
39" (99cm) of gold-filled
    24-gauge wire

TOOLS

Wire cutters
Flat-nose pliers
Round-nose pliers
Chain-nose pliers
Crimping pliers

FINISHED SIZE

15½" (39cm)

1   Use 3" (8cm) of 24-gauge wire and the largest briolette to form a wrapped loop bail that attaches to the bottom hole of one of the twig links. Repeat four times, using the largest briolettes, and attaching wrapped loop bails to the four holes on the sides of the link. Set aside.

2   Use wire cutters to cut two of the side holes off of each of the remaining twig links, making sure to cut the holes from the same side of each link.

3 Use 3" (8cm) of 24-gauge wire and one of the largest remaining briolettes to form a wrapped loop bail that attaches to one side hole of 1 twig link. Repeat to attach another briolette and wrapped loop bail to the other hole of the link. Repeat entire step with the 3 remaining twig links.

4 Use 3" (8cm) of beading wire to string 1 crimp tube and the top hole of the twig link used in Step 1. String 5 of the smallest briolettes, 1 crimp tube, and the bottom hole of 1 bird link. Pass back through the tube and crimp.

5 Repeat Step 4, attaching the first end of wire to the top hole of the bird link and the second end of wire to the bottom hole of a second twig link.

6 Repeat Step 4, attaching the first end of wire to the top hole of the twig link used in Step 5 and the second end of wire to a third twig link.

7 Use 4" (10cm) of beading wire to string 1 crimp tube and the top hole of the third twig link. String 9 of the smallest briolettes, 1 crimp tube, and the bar half of the clasp. Pass back through the tube and crimp.

8 Use 3" (8cm) of beading wire to string 1 crimp tube and the top hole of the twig link used in Step 1. String 5 of the smallest briolettes, 1 crimp tube, and the bottom hole of a fourth twig link.

9 Repeat Step 8, attaching the first end of wire to the top hole of the fourth twig link and the second end of wire to the bottom hole of the second bird link.

10 Repeat Step 8, attaching the first end of wire to the top hole of the bird link and the second end of wire to the bottom hole of the remaining twig link.

11 Repeat Step 7, attaching the first end of wire to the top of the twig link and the second half of wire to the ring half of the clasp.

TINY GEMS

Because of its association with peace, lapis lazuli has been a favored stone to use in carved images of the Buddha. The stone was also believed to be a protection against the evil eye. Lapis has been used in Western religious objects as well.

Earth and Sky

Long chrysoprase drops, cut to include the earth around them, become elegant earrings with the peyote bails stitched to the top. The color of chrysoprase is cool and airy, allowing the wearer to keep her head in the clouds without forgetting to keep her feet on the ground.

MATERIALS

About 50 color-lined metallic
  mustard AB size 15° seed
  beads (A)

About 150 bronze matte size 15°
  seed beads (B)

About 200 dark mint metal
  matte size 15° seed beads (C)

2 chrysoprase 8x40mm drops

1 pair sterling silver hoop
  earring findings

Beige Nymo size D
  beading thread

TOOLS

Scissors

Size 13 beading needle

Thread conditioner

FINISHED SIZE

3" (8cm)

1 Use 8" (20cm) of conditioned beading thread to string 4B and 1 drop, leaving a 4" (10cm) tail. Pass through all beads again (Figure 1). String 4B and pass through the drop (Figure 2). Pass through all the B again to join them into a ring (Figure 3).

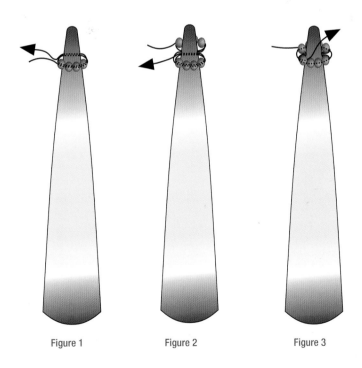

Figure 1   Figure 2   Figure 3

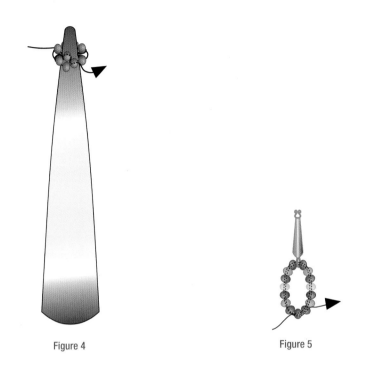

Figure 4

Figure 5

2 Use the working end of the thread to string 1B, skip the next B in the previous row, and pass through 1B in the previous row (Figure 4). Continue working peyote stitch and adding B around the row, working up toward the tip of the drop (see Techniques, page 113).

3 Work 5 rows of peyote stitch using mostly B beads, but adding a few A beads in randomly to add a bit of sparkle, and decreasing as necessary in order to keep close to the taper of the drop. When you finish the final row that covers the very tip of the drop, pass through the beads in that row again and exit from the B bead closest to the tip of the drop.

4 String 1B, 1A, 1B, 1C, 1B, 1A, 1B, the loop of one earring finding, 1B, 1A, 1B, 1C, 1B, 1A, and 1B. Pass through the B bead at the tip of the drop and pass through all the beads just strung again. Pass through the B bead at the tip of the drop and the first B strung in this step (Figure 5).

5 String 1C and pass through the second B strung in Step 4. String 1A and pass through the next B strung in Step 4. String 1C and pass through the next B, the loop of the earring finding, and the next B. String 1C and pass through the next B. String 1A and pass through the next B. String 1C and pass through the next B and the B at the tip of the drop (Figure 6).

Figure 6

6 String 2B and pass through the first C strung in Step 5. String 1B and pass through the first A strung in Step 5. String 2B and pass through the next C. Pass through the B, the loop of the earring finding, the B, and the next C. String 2B and pass through the next A. String 1B and pass through the next C. String 2B and pass through the B at the tip of the drop. Pass through the beads in the outer loop again to strengthen (Figure 7). Weave the thread back down through the beads at the top of the drop. Tie a couple of knots to secure the thread and trim.

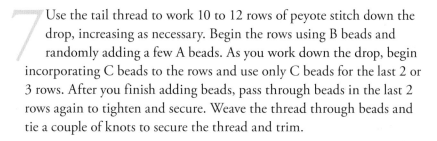

Figure 7

7 Use the tail thread to work 10 to 12 rows of peyote stitch down the drop, increasing as necessary. Begin the rows using B beads and randomly adding a few A beads. As you work down the drop, begin incorporating C beads to the rows and use only C beads for the last 2 or 3 rows. After you finish adding beads, pass through beads in the last 2 rows again to tighten and secure. Weave the thread through beads and tie a couple of knots to secure the thread and trim.

8 Repeat Steps 1–7 for the second earring.

TINY GEMS
In North America, Colorado's Mount Antero (14,269 ft.) is the highest source of gemstones—aquamarines in particular—and is accessible to collectors only two or three months each year.

Majestic Crests

Every kingdom has a crest, and it is widely known that purple is the color of royalty. Whether you're the queen or just queen for a day, these elegant earrings with different shapes of deep purple lepidolite are just what you need to feel regal.

1 Use wire cutters to cut the heads off of all head pins.

2 Use 1 head pin to string 1 lepidolite dangle to the center of the wire. Bend both ends of wire 90° toward the back of the dangle (Figure 1). Use both ends of wire to center the dangle on top of one filigree (Figure 2). Use your fingers to twist both ends of wire together behind the crest. Bend the wires down (Figure 3).

Figure 1

Figure 2

Figure 3

3 Place a second filigree back to back with the filigree used in Step 2. Use 1 ear wire to attach the filigrees at their tops.

4 Use 1 head pin to string 1 lepidolite briolette. Form a wrapped loop bail that attaches to the bottom hole of both filigrees. Repeat to attach 1 briolette to the bottom right corner of both filigrees. Repeat to attach 1 briolette to the bottom left corner of both filigrees.

5 Repeat Steps 2–4 to make the second earring.

TINY GEMS

Heat-treated gems aren't a strictly modern phenomenon. In ancient India, gems were sometimes cooked over a fire, a practice advocated in the two-thousand-year-old sacred text, Puranas.

did you know . . .

Peridot, Jewel of the Island of Serpents

While peridot has enjoyed recent popularity as a semiprecious stone, it was once regarded as among the most precious of stones. Included in Moses's list of twelve sacred stones, peridot was set in some of the world's most prestigious objects. A fabulous example of this is the Gold Festival Throne, which is housed in the Topkapi Palace Museum in Istanbul. A whopping 957 peridot stones are set in the gold-plated wood throne, a gift to Murad III in 1585 by his new son-in-law to celebrate the Ottoman colonization of Egypt. For ancients, the sole source of this beautiful green volcanic crystal was a small island in the Red Sea—called variously the Island of Serpents, Island of the Dead, and St. John's Island—located in Egypt. Pharaohs, and later the Ptolemies of Alexandria, guarded the island carefully from both intruders and from escape by the island's inhabitants. Today this once-legendary island, now called Zabargad Island, is desolate and all but forgotten. In its stead, the San Carlos Apache Reservation in Arizona provides nearly 90 percent of the world's supply of peridot.

The fabulous Topkapi Throne in Istanbul is encrusted with peridots. Courtesy of Philippe Giraud/Corbis Sygma

fashion-forward

Your best friend always knows the latest, greatest performance art events in town. Lucky for you, you are at the top of her invitation list. You both love dance, and this evening you will see an avant-garde group who combines athleticism with graceful surprise—all to the beat of Afro-Latin music.

Let's face it: Dramatic, expressive events inspire a little drama in each of us. And what better way to make a bold individual statement than to wear jewelry with spirit. Whether you are wearing a belted long silk shirt with fitted, dressy jeans and heels or a flirty, flowing dress, you'll want to pick your jewels and then flaunt them.

In today's bead market, you have some great options. How about a necklace made of African rough-cut sapphires, mixed with sunstone, topped off with beautiful raku ceramic blossoms as a focal element. Or maybe your idea of a **Fashion-Forward** accessory is an asymmetrical necklace with a multicolored glass focal bead, complemented by amethyst, serpentine, and carnelian "stone soup." Thanks to the many available stones that come in myriad shapes and finishes, you have an artist's palette from which to choose.

Mixing a rich collection of stones with a dramatic clasp and crystal accents can make a bracelet that says everything. And if you find artistic earring findings, like the scrolls in a design in this section, you won't need to do much other than wire-wrap some cool gaspeite and vesuvianite stones to give it a sassy but elegant edge.

Stone Soup

Anchored by a faceted glass focal bead resembling a geode, bright colors of amethyst, carnelian, and serpentine mix together in this festive piece. Beaders are sometimes stumped at how to design with a focal bead of this shape. This necklace is a fun design solution, as the large stones in the single strand of serpentine are balanced by four strands of smaller stones.

MATERIALS

188 carnelian 3x4mm teardrops
106 amethyst 6x4mm pebbles
22 serpentine 6x10mm pebbles
12 serpentine 8x10mm pebbles
1 borosilicate (boro) glass
    18x45mm faceted oval
50 black silver 4–6mm irregularly
    shaped spacers
1 black silver 14x55mm hook-and-
    eye clasp
7 black silver 2mm crimp tubes
1 sterling silver 4mm crimp tube
78" (2m) of silver .014
    beading wire

TOOLS

Wire cutters
Crimping pliers
Mighty Crimper crimping pliers

FINISHED SIZE

18½" (47cm)

1 Cut the beading wire into five 16" (41cm) pieces and one 10" (25cm) piece. Use all five 16" (41cm) pieces of wire to string the 4mm crimp tube. Pass the wires back through the tube, leaving a small loop, and crimp using the Mighty Crimper crimping pliers. Use the 10" (25cm) piece of wire to string 1 black crimp tube and the loop of wire just formed. Pass back through the tube and crimp using crimping pliers.

2 Use the 10" (25cm) wire to string the boro bead, hiding the loops of wire and crimp tubes from Step 1 inside the boro bead. Use the 10" (25cm) wire to string 1 spacer and 3 serpentine 8×10mm pebbles four times. String 1 spacer, 1 crimp tube, and the hook half of the clasp. Pass back through the tube, check to make sure the boro bead is concealing the crimps formed in Step 1, and crimp.

3 Use all five 16" (41cm) wires to string 1 spacer. Use 1 wire to string 3 carnelian teardrops (pointed end first), 1 spacer, 1 serpentine 6×10mm pebble, 1 spacer, 5 carnelian, 1 spacer, 1 serpentine 6×10mm, 1 spacer, 7 carnelian, 1 spacer, 1 serpentine 6×10mm, 1 spacer, 9 carnelian, 1 spacer, 1 serpentine 6×10mm, 38 carnelian, 1 crimp tube, and the eye half of the clasp. Pass back through the tube and crimp.

4 Use 1 wire to string 5 amethyst pebbles, 1 spacer, 1 serpentine 6×10mm, and 1 spacer five times. String 30 amethyst, 1 crimp tube, and the eye half of the clasp. Pass back through the tube and crimp.

5 Use 1 wire to string 8 carnelian, 1 spacer, 1 serpentine 6×10mm, and 1 spacer. String 7 carnelian, 1 spacer, 1 serpentine 6×10mm, and 1 spacer three times. String 35 carnelian, 1 crimp tube, and the eye half of the clasp. Pass back through the tube and crimp.

6 Use 1 wire to string 5 amethyst, 1 spacer, 1 serpentine 6×10mm, and 1 spacer five times. String 26 amethyst, 1 crimp tube, and the eye half of the clasp. Pass back through the tube and crimp.

7 Use 1 wire to string 9 carnelian, 1 spacer, 1 serpentine 6×10mm, 1 spacer, 7 carnelian, 1 spacer, 1 serpentine 6×10mm, 1 spacer, 5 carnelian, 1 spacer, 1 serpentine 6×10mm, 1 spacer, 3 carnelian, 1 spacer, 1 serpentine 6×10mm, 1 spacer, 38 carnelian, 1 crimp tube, and the eye half of the clasp. Pass back through the tube and crimp.

TINY GEMS

Renaissance genius Leonardo da Vinci claimed, "Amethyst dissipates evil thoughts and quickens the intelligence."

83

did you know . . .

Carnelian through the Ages

Throughout time, carnelian has symbolized many different things. Ancient Egyptians, who thought the stone brought protection in the afterlife, placed a carnelian amulet on the body of the deceased. In medieval Europe, carnelian's healing attributes were believed to be its ability to calm one and still the blood. It was also seen as a stone that imparted courage. In the 1700s, carnelian was said to bring luck, protection, and comfort. And in the 1800s, carnelian was said to help those who needed courage to speak. By wearing carnelian, anyone who was shy or had a weak voice could speak boldly and well. Mohammed, Napoleon I, and Napoleon III are a few of the historic figures who wore carnelian.

Raku Princess

Raku, a form of pottery dating back to sixteenth-century Japan, is unique due in part to its firing process and the fact that the colors and patterns of the glazes are unpredictable. Sapphire and sunstone, when combined with raku flowers, form a sparkling necklace fit for royalty.

MATERIALS

8 sunstone 9x10mm rectangles

26 sapphire 16mm nuggets

8 raku 20mm ceramic flowers

1 sterling silver 15mm button with shank

83 Thai silver 2x3mm rondelles

3 sterling silver 9mm 3-link chains

2 sterling silver 2x3mm crimp tubes

24" (61cm) of silver .019 beading wire

35" (89cm) of sterling silver 22-gauge wire

TOOLS

Wire cutters

Chain-nose pliers

Flat-nose pliers

Round-nose pliers

Crimping pliers

FINISHED SIZE

18½" (47cm)

1 Use 5" (13cm) of 22-gauge wire to string 1 raku flower. Place the flower at about the 3" (8cm) mark of the wire and bend both ends up around the flower (Figure 1). Use the shorter end of the wire to wrap around the longer end, coiling once (Figure 2). Trim the short end of wire. Use the long end of wire to string 1 rondelle. Form a wrapped loop, with the loop parallel to the wire around the flower (Figure 3). Repeat entire step for a total of 4 flower dangles.

Figure 1   Figure 2   Figure 3

Figure 4

2 Repeat Step 1, making the wrapped loop perpendicular to the wire around the flower and attaching the loop to 1 chain prior to wrapping (Figure 4). Repeat to make 3 chain dangles.

3 Use the beading wire to string 1 crimp tube, 1 flower, and the button. Pass back through the flower and the tube, and crimp. String 1 sapphire nugget and 1 rondelle thirteen times. String 1 sunstone rectangle, 1 rondelle, 1 flower dangle, 1 rondelle, 1 rectangle, and 1 chain dangle three times. String 1 rectangle, 1 rondelle, 1 flower dangle, 1 rondelle, and 1 rectangle. String 1 rondelle and 1 nugget thirteen times. String 1 crimp tube and 42 rondelles. Pass back through the tube, snug the beads, make sure the loop of rondelles fits around the button and flower, and crimp.

TINY GEMS

The ancient Persians believed that the earth rested on a giant sapphire, which spread its deep blue color throughout the universe.

Central Attraction

Shades of brown and green complement each other well in this attractive, earthy creation. The shiny dots on the matte topaz briolettes are the perfect accompaniment to the sandblasted focal bead at the center of it all.

MATERIALS

56 olive metallic size 15° seed beads

60 chocolate matte opaque size 11° seed beads

38 Afghan jade 2x3mm tubes

27 topaz matte with shiny dots 12mm briolettes

1 brown and green honeycomb 25mm sandblasted borosilicate (boro) glass focal bead

4 natural brass 6mm jump rings

2 natural brass 9.5mm etched jump rings

1 natural brass 20mm toggle ring

3 natural brass 2mm crimp tubes

1 natural brass 4x25mm bead pod toggle bar

2 natural brass 20mm hammered toggle rings

1 natural brass 2" (5cm) head pin

22" (56cm) bronze .019 beading wire

TOOLS

Wire cutters

Flat-nose pliers

Chain-nose pliers

Round-nose pliers

Crimping pliers

FINISHED SIZE

16½" (42cm)

1 Use 2" (5cm) of beading wire to string 1 topaz briolette. Use both ends of wire to string 1 crimp tube. Slide the tube toward the briolette, leaving about ¼" (.6cm) of wire between the tube and each side of the briolette. Crimp the tube and trim the tails (Figure 1).

Figure 1

2 Use wire cutters to cut the flat end off the head pin, leaving 2" (5cm) of wire. Use one end of wire to form a tiny wrapped loop that attaches to the piece formed in Step 1 (Figure 2). Use chain-nose pliers to flatten the loop so that it will fit through the bottom hole of the focal bead (Figure 3). Use the head pin to string the focal bead, making sure the briolette hangs evenly beneath the focal bead, and form a wrapped loop. Set aside.

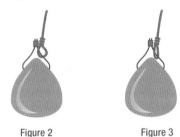

Figure 2   Figure 3

3 Use one 6mm jump ring to attach the 2 toggle rings. Use 1 etched jump ring to attach the 6mm jump ring on the toggle rings to a second 6mm jump ring. Set aside. Attach one 6mm jump ring to the toggle bar. Use 1 etched jump ring to attach the 6mm jump ring on the toggle bar to a fourth 6mm jump ring. Fold open one end of the toggle bar. Insert 8 jade tubes into the bar and close the end.

4 Use 20" (51cm) beading wire to string 1 crimp tube, 1 size 11° seed bead, and the 6mm jump ring at the end of one half of the clasp. Pass back through the size 11° and the tube and crimp. String 1 size 15°, 1 size 11°, 1 jade tube, 1 size 11°, 1 size 15°, and 1 briolette fourteen times, omitting the final briolette. String 1 size 11° and 1 jade tube.

5 String the pendant formed in Steps 1 and 2. Repeat Step 4, reversing the stringing sequence, and attaching the wire to the jump ring on the end of the other half of the clasp.

TINY GEMS

In Mesoamerican cultures, jade grave objects were considered essential for the nobility. To ensure they would accompany their owner beyond the grave, the jade objects were often broken or "killed." Also, a piece of jade was placed in the mouth of a deceased noble to serve as a heart in the afterlife.

Amethyst d'Amore

MATERIALS

27 amethyst gold luster
    size 15° seed beads (A)
41 clear champagne-lined
    size 15° seed beads (B)
19 purple gold/amethyst-lined
    size 15° seed beads (C)
103 purple gold metallic iris
    size 12° charlottes (D)
18 clear sparkling sand-lined
    size 10° Delicas (E)
21 smoked amethyst matte
    AB size 10° Delicas (F)
27 amethyst 6mm faceted
    rondelles
1 raku ceramic 20mm coin
1 raku ceramic 20mm
    square coin
8 gold-filled 2mm crimp tubes
1 gold-filled 22-gauge
    2" (5cm) head pin
31" (79cm) of purple .019
    beading wire

TOOLS

Wire cutters
Flat-nose pliers
Round-nose pliers
Chain-nose pliers
Magical Crimp Forming pliers

FINISHED SIZE

7" (18cm)

Even a short strand of fancy faceted amethyst looks lush when mixed with seed beads. Seed beads in different sizes and colors bring out the rainbow of colors in the raku ceramic coins, which serve not only as a clasp but also as focal piece in this bracelet. With a design like this, who couldn't love amethyst?

1 Attach 7" (18cm) of beading wire to the left side of the square coin using a crimp tube. String 5 rondelles, 1 crimp tube, and 38D. Pass back through the tube and crimp.

2 Use the head pin to string 1 rondelle, the coin, and 1 rondelle. Form a 4mm wrapped loop.

3 Use 12" (31cm) of beading wire to string the right side of the square coin. Use both ends of wire to string 1 crimp tube. Center the coin on the wire, snug the tube, and crimp.

4 Use 1 wire to string 3B. String 1A, 1 rondelle, 1A, 5D, 3B, and 5D three times. String 1A, 1 rondelle, 1A, 1 crimp tube, and the wrapped loop formed in Step 2. Pass back through the tube and crimp.

5 Use the other wire to string 5C. String 3F, 1B, 1 rondelle, and 1B seven times. String 1 crimp tube and the wrapped loop. Pass back through the tube and crimp.

6 Repeat Step 3.

7 Use 1 wire to string 6A and 7D. String 1B, 1 rondelle, 1B, 7D, 6A, and 7D twice. String 1 crimp tube and the wrapped loop. Pass back through the tube and crimp.

8 Use the remaining wire to string 5B, 1C, 1 rondelle, and 1C. String 3E, 1C, 1 rondelle, and 1C six times. String 1 crimp tube and the wrapped loop. Pass back through the tube and crimp.

did you know . . .

The Virtue of Amethyst

This popular semiprecious stone was named for a young woman desired by the Greek god Dionysus, god of wine and fecundity. The mortal woman spurned the Olympian, choosing instead to worship the goddess Diana. Angered by the rejection, Dionysus ordered two tigers to devour her, but Diana intervened and turned the pure maiden into white quartz. Dionysus shed tears over the outcome of his reckless passion, tears that fell into his goblet of red wine. Some of the wine spilled over onto the white quartz, which absorbed its color and became the purple stone amethyst.

Captured Carnelian

Square-stitched rings in two colorways are the perfect accessory for gorgeous faceted carnelian rondelles. Mimicking the picot edging on the rings is the clasp loop, which brings all the colors together and completes this chunky bracelet.

MATERIALS

234 topaz matte silver-lined size 15° seed beads (A)

171 rosy topaz gold luster size 15° seed beads (B)

538 rosy topaz matte silver-lined size 11° seed beads (C)

350 rusty orange-lined size 11° seed beads (D)

24 carnelian 7x14mm faceted rondelles

Crystal FireLine 6lb line

Orange size D Nymo beading thread

TOOLS

Scissors

Size 12 beading needles

Thread conditioner

FINISHED SIZE

8½" (22cm)

1 Use square stitch to make a strip of C beads 8 beads wide by 20 rows long. Use 8' (2m) of FireLine to string a tension bead, leaving an 8" (20cm) tail.

Row 1: String 8C.

Row 2: String 1C. Pass through the last bead of the previous row and the bead just strung (Figure 1). String 1C and pass through the next bead of the previous row and the bead just strung (Figure 2). Repeat for the length of the row, stitching 1 new bead to each bead of the previous row.

Rows 3–20: Repeat Row 2.

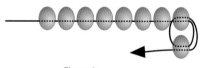

Figure 1

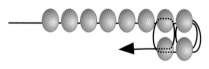

Figure 2

2 Stitch the strip into a ring: With the thread exiting the last bead of Row 20, pass through the last bead of Row 1 and the last bead of Row 20. Repeat for the length of the row, connecting each bead of Row 1 to its match in Row 20 (Figure 3).

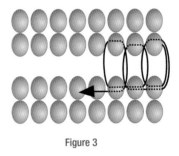

Figure 3

3 Add a picot edge to the ring: With the thread exiting from one end of the ring, string 3A and pass down through all of the beads in the next row. String 3 beads again and pass down through all of the beads in the next row (Figure 4). Continue around the ring. When you reach the final row, pass through the row of C and the first A bead strung. String 1A and, working in the opposite direction, pass down through the next A and the row of C (Figure 5). Repeat around the ring until there is a picot at both ends of every row.

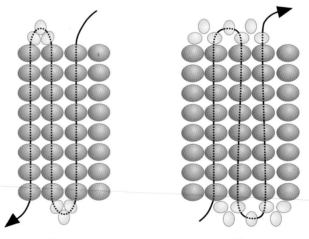

Figure 4   Figure 5

4 Repeat Steps 1–3 twice more using C and A beads. Repeat Steps 1–3 twice using D and B beads.

5 Use 5' (2m) of beading thread on a beading needle to string 1D. Leave a 6" (15cm) tail and tie a square knot around the D. String 1 carnelian rondelle, 1B, and 1C. String 1B and 1 rondelle three times.

6 Place 1 rondelle inside 1 C and A ring. String the rondelle/ring by passing the needle between the fourth and fifth C beads of one row, through the rondelle, and between the fourth and fifth C beads on the other side of the ring.

7 String 1 rondelle and 1B twice. String 1 rondelle. Repeat Step 6, using 1 D and B ring. String 1 rondelle and 1B twice. Repeat entire step three times, alternating C and A and D and B rings.

8 String 1 rondelle and 1B twice. String 1 rondelle, 1D, 1B, and 29C. Pass back through the B and all of the beads in the bracelet, including the first D strung. Use the working and tail threads to tie and surgeon's knot. Skip the D and pass through all the beads in the strand, including the loop of C at the end of the bracelet.

9 Pass through 1C of the loop. String 1C, 1D, and 1C. Pass the needle through the loop and back through the C just strung, making sure the thread passes between the first and second C of the loop (Figure 6). *String 1D and 1C. Pass the needle through the loop between the previous and the next C of the loop, and back through the C just strung. Repeat from * all around the loop.

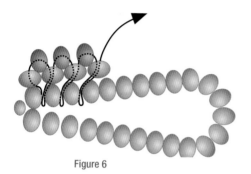

Figure 6

Asian Scrolls

Scroll-like chandelier pieces are the perfect accent for vesuvianite briolette "fans." The veining in the gaspeite rondelles brings the colors together. The five dangles represent a Japanese design rule of always using odd numbers.

MATERIALS

6 gaspeite 4x6mm rondelles

6 vesuvianite 8mm faceted briolettes

2 brown 25mm filigree shell chandelier pieces

18 gold-filled 2mm rounds

1 pair gold-filled French ear wires

4 gold-filled 2" (5cm) head pins

24" (61cm) of gold-filled 24-gauge wire

TOOLS

Wire cutters

Flat-nose pliers

Chain-nose pliers

Round-nose pliers

FINISHED SIZE

3" (8cm)

1 Use 3" (8cm) of wire and 1 briolette to form a wrapped loop bail. Use the tail end of wire to string 1 round and form a wrapped loop that attaches to the middle loop of the bottom of 1 chandelier piece.

2 Use 1 head pin to string 1 round, 1 rondelle, and 1 round. Form a wrapped loop that attaches to one loop on the side of the middle loop of the chandelier piece. Repeat Step for the loop on the other side of the middle loop.

3 Repeat Step 1 for the remaining loops on the bottom of the chandelier piece.

4 Use 3" (8cm) of wire to form a wrapped loop that attaches to the top of the chandelier piece. String 1 round, 1 rondelle, and 1 round and form a wrapped loop that attaches to 1 ear wire.

5 Repeat Steps 1–4 for the second earring.

Soaring at Sunrise

Red coral coins represent the deep red sun that rises in the sky at daybreak. The little brass bird is off to catch the worm and the brass connector with its delicate pattern adds the perfect finishing touch to this fun pair of earrings.

MATERIALS

2 coral 12mm coins

2 natural brass bird charms

2 natural brass 2-hole deco
   window connectors

1 pair natural brass ear wires

2 natural brass 2" (5cm)
   head pins

TOOLS

Wire cutters

Flat-nose pliers

Round-nose pliers

Chain-nose pliers

FINISHED SIZE

2½" (6cm)

1 Use wire cutters to cut off the head of each head pin.

2 Use 1 head pin to form a wrapped loop that attaches to 1 bird charm. String 1 coral coin. Form a wrapped loop that attaches to the bottom of 1 connector.

3 Attach 1 ear wire to the top of the connector.

4 Repeat Steps 2 and 3 for the second earring.

techniques
and findings

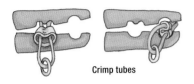
Crimp tubes

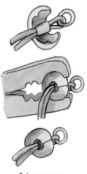
Crimp covers

Crimping

Crimp tubes are seamless tubes of metal that come in several sizes. To use, string a crimp tube through the connection finding. Pass back through the tube, leaving a short tail. Use the back notch of the crimping pliers to press the length of the tube down between the wires, enclosing them in separate chambers of the crescent shape. Rotate the tube 90° and use the front notch of the pliers to fold the two chambers onto themselves, forming a clean cylinder. Trim the excess wire.

Crimp covers hide a 2mm crimp tube and give a professional finish. To attach, gently hold a crimp cover in the front notch of the crimping pliers. Insert the crimped tube and gently squeeze the pliers, encasing the tube inside the cover.

Finishing and Starting New Threads

Tie off your old thread when it's about 4" (10cm) long by making a simple knot between beads. Pass through a few beads and pull tight to hide the knot. Weave through a few more beads and trim the thread close to the work. Start the new thread by tying a knot between beads and weaving through a few beads. Pull tight to hide the knot. Weave through several beads until you reach the place to resume beading.

Jump Rings

Open a jump ring by grasping each side of its opening with a pair of pliers. Don't pull apart. Instead, twist in opposite directions so that you can open and close without distorting the shape.

Knots

Half-Hitch Knot

Half-hitch knots may be worked with two or more strands—one strand is knotted over one or more other strands. Form a loop around the cord(s). Pull the end through the loop just formed and pull tight. Repeat for the length of cord you want to cover.

Half-hitch knot

Overhand Knot

The overhand knot is the basic knot for tying off thread. Make a loop with the stringing material. Pass the cord that lies behind the loop over the front cord and through the loop. Pull tight.

Overhand knot

Square Knot

The square knot is the classic sturdy knot for securing most stringing materials. First make an overhand knot, passing the right end over the left end. Next, make another overhand knot, this time passing the left end over the right end. Pull tight.

Square knot

Surgeon's Knot

The surgeon's knot is very secure and therefore good for finishing off most stringing materials. Tie an overhand knot, right over left, but instead of one twist over the left cord, make at least two. Tie another overhand knot, left over right, and pull tight.

Surgeon's knot

Pass Through vs Pass Back Through

"Pass through" means to move your needle in the same direction that the beads have been strung. "Pass back through" means to move your needle in the opposite direction.

Stitches

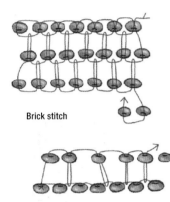

Brick stitch

Brick-stitch decrease

Brick Stitch

Begin by creating a foundation row in ladder stitch or using a secured thread. String 2 beads and pass under the closest exposed loop of the foundation row and back through the second bead. String 1 bead and pass under the next exposed loop and back through the bead just strung; repeat.

To decrease within a row, string 1 bead and skip a loop of thread on the previous row, passing under the second loop and back through the bead.
To increase within a row, work 2 stitches in the same loop on the previous row.

Herringbone Stitch

Begin with a foundation row of even-count ladder stitch. String 2 beads, pass down through the second-to-last bead in the ladder, and up through the next bead. String 2 beads, pass down the next bead and then up through the following. Repeat to the end of the row. To end the row, pass back through the last bead strung. To begin the next row, string 2 beads and pass down through the second to last bead of the previous row and up through the following bead. Repeat, stringing 2 beads per stitch and passing down then up through 2 beads of the previous row. The 2-bead stitch will cause the beads to angle-up in each row, like a herringbone fabric.

Herringbone stitch

Ladder Stitch

Using two needles, one threaded on each side of the thread, pass 1 needle through 1 or more beads from the left to the right, and pass the other needle through the same beads from the left to the right. Continue adding beads by crisscrossing both needles through each bead or group of beads. Use ladder stitch to make strings of beads or to lay the foundation for brick or herringbone stitch.

For a single-needle ladder, string 2 beads and pass through them again. String 1 bead. Pass through the last stitched bead and the one just strung. Repeat, adding 1 bead at a time and working in a figure-eight pattern.

Ladder stitch (double needle)

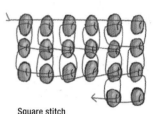

Ladder stitch (single needle)

Square Stitch

Begin by stringing a row of beads. For the second row, string 2 beads, pass through the second-to-last bead of the first row, and back through the second bead of those just strung. Continue by stringing 1 bead, passing through the third-to-last bead of the first row, and back through the bead just strung. Repeat this looping technique to the end of the row.

To make a decrease, weave thread through the previous row and exit from the bead adjacent to the place you want to decrease. Continue working in square stitch.
To make an increase, string the number of beads at the end of the row you want to increase. Work the next row the same as the previous row.

Square stitch

Tubular Peyote Stitch

To make a mid-project decrease, simply pass thread through 2 beads without adding a bead in the "gap." In the next row, work a regular one-drop peyote over the decrease. Keep tension taut to avoid holes.

To make a mid-project increase, work a two-drop over a one-drop in one row. In the next row, work a one-drop peyote between the two-drop. For a smooth increase, use very narrow beads for both the two-drop and the one-drop between.

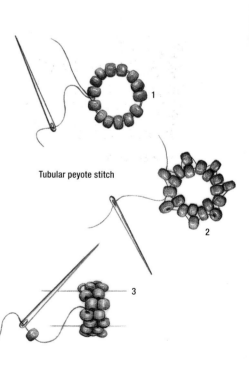

Tubular peyote stitch

Stringing

Stringing is a technique in which you use a beading wire, needle and thread, or other material to gather beads into a strand.

Stringing

Tension Bead

String a bead larger than those you are working with, then pass through the bead one or more times, making sure not to split your thread. The bead will be able to slide along but will still provide tension to work against when you're beading the first 2 rows.

Tension bead

Wireworking

Simple Loop

To form a simple loop, use flat-nose pliers to make a 90° bend at least ½" (1cm) from the end of the wire. Use round-nose pliers to grasp the wire after the bend; roll the pliers toward the bend, but not past it, to preserve the 90° bend. Use your thumb to continue the wrap around the nose of the pliers. Trim the wire next to the bend. Open a simple loop by grasping each side of its opening with a pair of pliers. Don't pull apart. Instead, twist in opposite directions so that you can open and close without distorting the shape.

Simple loop

Wrapped Loop

To form a wrapped loop, begin with a 90° bend at least 2" (5cm) from the end of the wire. Use round-nose pliers to form a simple loop with a tail overlapping the bend. Wrap the tail tightly down the neck of the wire to create a couple of coils. Trim the excess wire to finish. Make a double wrapped loop by wrapping the wire back up over the coils, toward the loop, and trimming at the loop. Link a wrapped loop to another loop by passing the wire through the previous loop before wrapping the neck of the new loop.

Wrapped loop

Wrapped-Loop Bails

Wrapped bails turn side-drilled beads, usually teardrops, into pendants. Center the bead on a 6" (15cm) piece of wire. Bend both ends of the wire up the sides and across the top of the bead. Bend one end straight up at the center of the bead and wrap the other wire around it to form a few coils. Form a wrapped loop with the straight-up wire, wrapping it back down over the already-formed coils. Trim the excess wire.

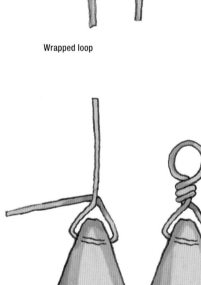

Wrapped-loop bail

PROJECT RESOURCES

Materials

Amethyst d'Amore, 94
Seed beads: Beyond Beadery
Amethyst: Artgems, Inc.
Raku ceramic coins: Rama with
  Emerald's Beads
Wire: Soft Flex Company

Arachne's Treasure, 62
Blue apatite rondelles and coins:
  Dakota Stones
Hessonite garnet: Artgems, Inc.
Swarovski crystal bicones:
  Beyond Beadery
Clasp: Jess Imports

Asian Scrolls, 104
Gaspeite and vesuvianite: Artgems, Inc.
Shell chandelier pieces, ear wires, 2mm
  rounds, and wire: Fusion Beads

Captured Carnelian, 98
Seed beads: Beyond Beadery
Carnelian: Artgems, Inc.

Central Attraction, 90
Size 15° seed beads: Jane's Fiber
  and Beads
Size 11° seed beads: Beyond Beadery
Jade tubes and bronze beading wire:
  Soft Flex Company
Topaz briolettes: Artgems, Inc.
Borosilicate focal bead: Jones Art Glass
Natural brass findings: Family Glass

Earth and Sky, 70
Seed beads: Out On A Whim
Chrysoprase drops: Artgems, Inc.
Earring findings: Nina Designs

Good Fortune, 24
Seed beads: Beyond Beadery
Aquamarine and imperial jasper:
  Bonita Creations
Scarab charm: Earthenwood Studio
Clasp: Via Murano

Heavenly Lotus, 56
Green amethyst marquis:
  Oriental GemCo
Lotus jasper: Zeka Beads
Pewter pendant: Green Girl Studios
Clasp: Under One Sun

Lucky Strike, 38
Red jade tubes and butterscotch wire:
  Soft Flex Company
Chalcedony: Artgems, Inc.
Toggle clasp: Jess Imports

Majestic Crests, 74
Lepidolite briolettes: Soft Flex Company
Lepidolite dangles: Two Cranes
Natural brass wire, filigree, and ear
  wires: Family Glass

Modern Art, 28
Onyx rounds: Fusion Beads
Onyx frames: MB Imports
Amazonite ovals: Dakota Stones
Black beading wire: Soft Flex Company

Opulent Cowgirl, 34
Smoky quartz: Dakota Stones
Muscovite and all turquoise: Elan
Clasp: Kipuka Trading

Raku Princess, 86
Sunstone and sapphire: Soft
  Flex Company
Raku flowers: Rama with Emerald Stacy
Button: Michelene A. Berkey
Rondelles: Somerset Silver
3-link chains: Singaraja

Ring of Sapphires, 40
Seed beads: Beyond Beadery
Sapphire briolettes: Artgems, Inc.
Carnelian pebbles: Bonita Creations
Clasp: Jess Imports

Sangria Dangles, 42
Pink garnet: Soft Flex Company
Tourmaline: Artgems, Inc.
VEE-O Vogue rings: Via Murano
Ear wires: Nina Designs
Head pins: The Bead Shop

Soaring at Sunrise, 106
Natural brass: Family Glass

Stone Soup, 80
Carnelian, amethyst, serpentine, 4mm
  crimp tube, beading wire, and Mighty
  Crimper crimping pliers: Soft Flex
  Company
Borosilicate glass faceted oval:
  Family Glass

Black silver irregularly shaped spacers,
  clasp, and crimp tubes: Shiana

Swinging Mosaics, 46
Gold coins and chain: Singaraja Imports

Temple in the Clouds, 22
Peach moonstone: Artgems, Inc.
Imperial jasper: Bonita Creations
Borosilicate glass rondelles and natural
  brass beads and findings: Family Glass
Butterscotch wire: Soft Flex Company

Tourmaline Sea, 32
Seed beads: Jane's Fiber and Beads
Tourmaline: Artgems, Inc.
Amazonite: Dakota Stones
Black sterling silver bamboo leaves,
  clasp, and findings: Shiana

Twilight Flight, 66
Lapis lazuli: Avian Oasis
Gold vermeil twig and bird links, clasp,
  24-gauge wire, and crimp tubes:
  Fusion Beads
24k gold beading wire: Soft Flex
  Company

Un, deux, trois!, 50
Lemon quartz rectangles: Artgems, Inc.
Chalcedony and agate: Zeka Beads
Chain, clasps, and figure eights:
  Fusion Beads

Vintage Vogue, 60
Blue apatite rondelles: Dakota Stones
Smoky Citrine: Avian Oasis
Natural brass beads, bead caps, toggle
  clasp, and findings: Family Glass
Bronze beading wire: Soft Flex
  Company

Sources

Artgems, Inc.
4860 East Baseline Road
Mesa, AZ 85206
(480) 545-6009
www.artgemsinc.com

Avian Oasis
1644 North 192nd Avenue
Buckeye, AZ 85396
(602) 571-3385
www.avianoasis.com

The Bead Shop
158 University Avenue
Palo Alto, CA 94301
(650) 328-7925
www.beadshop.com

Beyond Beadery
PO Box 460
Rollinsville, CO 80474
(800) 840-5548
www.beyondbeadery.com

Bokamo Designs
5609 West 99th Street
Overland Park, KS 66207
(913) 648-4296
www.bokamodesigns.com

Bonita Creations
3370 Arapahoe Avenue
Boulder, CO 80303
(310) 490-0548
www.bonitacreations.com

Dakota Stones
7279 Washington Avenue South
Edina, MN 55439
(866) 871-1990
www.dakotastones.com

Earthenwood Studio
PO Box 20002
Ferndale, MI 48220
earthenwood@comcast.net
www.earthenwoodstudio.com

Elan
Ellen Wells & Raj
2305-C Ashland Street #157
Ashland, OR 97520
(541) 488-2323
ellenwells@mac.com

Family Glass
3915 Elledge Drive
Roeland Park, KS 66205
(913) 231-1313
www.familyglass.com

Fusion Beads
3830 Stone Way North
Seattle, WA 98103
(888) 781-3559
www.fusionbeads.com

Green Girl Studios
PO Box 19389
Asheville, NC 28815
(828) 298-2263
www.greengirlstudios.com

Jane's Fiber and Beads
5415 East Andrew Johnson Highway
PO Box 110
Afton, TN 37616
(888) 497-2665
www.janesfiberandbeads.com

Jess Imports
(wholesale only)
110 Gough Street, Suite 203A
San Francisco, CA 94102
(415) 626-1433
www.jessimports.com

Jones Art Glass
Rashan Omari Jones
(505) 217-8535
JonesArtGlass@gmail.com
www.glassartists.org/jonesartglass

Kipuka Trading
200 Possum Trot
Liberty Hill, TX 78642
(512) 515-6605
www.kipukatrading.com

MB Imports
2442 NW Market Street #350
Seattle, WA 98107
(206) 374-9042
www.mbbeads.com

Nina Designs
PO Box 8127
Emeryville, CA 94662
(800) 336-6462
www.ninadesigns.com

Oriental GemCo.
56 W. 45th Street, 5th Floor
New York, NY 10036-4215
(212) 391-5801
www.orientalgemco.com

Out On A Whim
121 East Cotati Avenue
Cotati, CA US 94931
(800) 232-3111
www.whimbeads.com

Rama with Emerald's Beads
2411 Lincoln Avenue Southeast
Olympia, WA 98501
(360) 888-3404
emeraldstacy@hotmail.com
www.rama.citymax.com

Shiana
www.shiana.com

Singaraja Imports
PO Box 4624
Vineyard Haven, MA 02568
(800) 865-8856
www.singarajaimports.com

Soft Flex Company
PO Box 80
Sonoma, CA 95476
(866) 925-FLEX (3539)
www.softflexcompany.com

Somerset Silver
PO Box 253
Mukilteo, WA 98275
(425) 641-3666
www.somerset-silver.com

Tigress Design Studio
Michelene A. Berkey
(303) 670-8274
www.tigressdesignstudio.com

Two Cranes
PO Box 116
Socorro, NM 87801
www.2cranes.biz

Under One Sun
www.under-one-sun.com

Via Murano
17654 Newhope Street, Suite A
Fountain Valley, CA 92708
(877) VIAMURANO
www.viamurano.com

Zeka Beads
100 East 51st Street #7
Austin, TX 78751
(512) 206-0542
www.zekabeads.com

RELATED READING

For more beading designs and techniques, join the community at beadingdaily.com where life meets beading or subscribe to Interweave's beading magazines:

Beadwork
Step by Step Beads
Step by Step Wire Jewelry
Stringing

Bonewitz, Ronald Louis. *Rock and Gem*. New York: Dorling Kindersley, Inc., 2005.

Cipriani, Curzio, and Alessandro Borelli. *Simon & Schuster's Guide to Gems and Precious Stones*. New York: Simon & Schuster, 1986.

Dubin, Lois Sherr. *The History of Beads, from 30,000 B.C. to the Present*. New York: Harry N. Abrams, Inc., 1987.

Finlay, Victoria. *Jewels: A Secret History*. New York: Ballantine Books, 2006.

Hall, Cally. *Smithsonian Handbooks: Gemstones*. New York: Dorling Kindersley, Inc., 2002.

Voillot, Patrick. *Diamonds and Precious Stones*. New York: Harry N. Abrams, Inc., 1998.

INDEX

Sophisticated Jewelry Made So Simple

with these inspiring resources from Interweave

Are you **Beading Daily?**

Join **BeadingDaily.com**, an online community that shares your passion for beading. You'll get a free e-newsletter, free projects, a daily blog, a pattern store, galleries, artist interviews, contests, tips and techniques, event updates, and more.

Sign up for Beading Daily at beadingdaily.com

where life meets beading

INTERWEAVE™
interweave.com